Myths Unveiled

By Malik Bade

@ACENSIONRISE

Tables of Content

Chapter 1: The Sun of God 4

Chapter 2: Astrological Nature of the Bible 16

Chapter 3: Concealed Concepts of the Bible 43

Chapter 4: The Book of Revelation and Astrotheology (1) 48

Chapter 5: The Book of Revelation and Astrotheology (2) 56

Chapter 6: Unveiling the Alpha and Omega 65

Chapter 7: The God of 1000 Names 71

Chapter 8: Lunar Cults - Adoration or Veneration of the Moon 91

Chapter 9: Islam's Relationship With the Vatican and the Occult 102

Chapter 10: Legends, Myths, and Origins 110

Chapter 11: Mystery Babylonian Symbols - Extras 116

References 135

Introduction

For thousands of years, people have been debating and discussing religion. If anybody is familiar with me or my work, you will know that I believe the major modern religions have a deeper meaning that is far different from what the world's mainstream views or what we have been told.

People's belief on faith and religion in fact comes by an accident of geography, ingrained cultural heritages which shapes what life is viewed for the many millions to billions around the world. However, any critical thinker equipped with the means to delve deeply into the origins of many of the most well-known religious concepts would recognise a recurrent pattern and theme. From the so-called pagans to our contemporary worldviews, the same concepts are applied in various manners. Upon careful reflection, reading, and investigation of sources and reference materials from all directions, it became evident that many of the stories were not based on actual events. When you truly go into its origins, however, you will find that it comes from a higher spiritual meaning that describes esoteric messages. Such are observations of the sky, planets, stars, and time zones, which all play a part in the many stories that were circulated and burrowed throughout the course of history.

Everything that we have been told to be the truth about religion is just used to control the people. To keep the sheep aligned and far away from the rulers that be. Under the pretense of organized religious groups, holiness is being utilized as a front for sinister power that serves its creation's ultimate goal. People are slowly realizing that there is a false hope or that something isn't being talked about, which is an uncommon sensation of awakening. But most people are still far away from the truth or have been hardwired into ideas that have rendered them as mental captives. Religion will slowly decline with every generation; presently, it serves as a social structure for people of many cultures and societies. For the present being, it is essential to examine the unseen truth or a perspective that should be taken into consideration by anyone with an interest in fascinating and astounding connections. Patterns of thoughts and concepts used by the observable universe. As with all of my writings, one should read this with an open mind and remove any innate prejudices for better understanding. Religion is here to decipher the truth, not set it. Let's begin by unraveling the world's most profound mysteries.

Chapter 1: The Sun of God

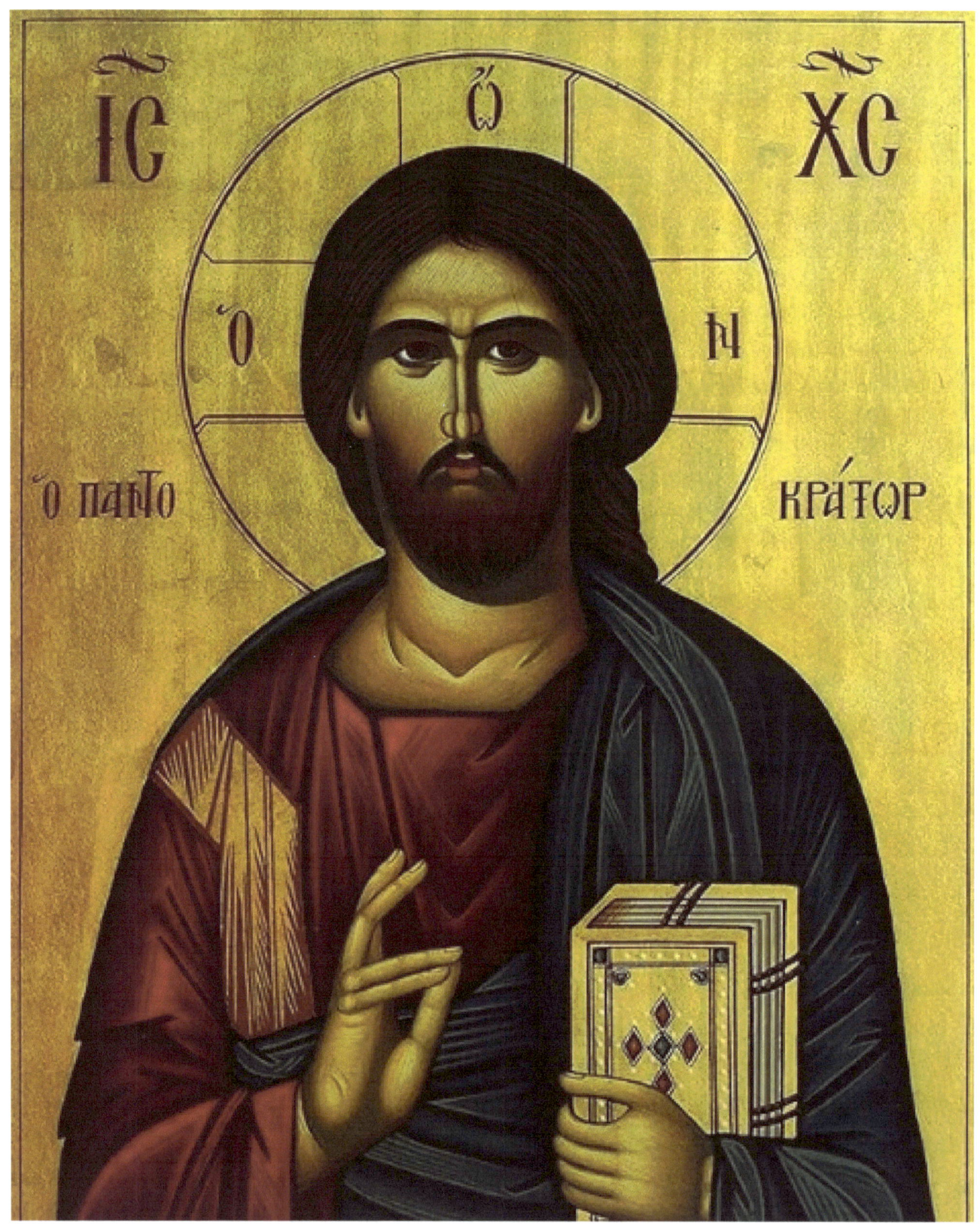

Current Consensus of Christianity and Historical Evidence

The Roman execution of Jesus will mostly be attributed to the fact that a Jewish preacher named Jesus was tried, found guilty, and laid to execution. However, given that these assertions were made more than a century after Christianity was a recognised sect, such evidence cannot be anymore unreliable. Our sources are secondary, based on claims made by historians decades after the alleged crucifixion, with no contemporary sources and no tangible evidence outside of the Bible. Although mainstream scholars start with the arbitrary assumption that Jesus had to have existed, they have no concrete evidence to back up their assertions. Therefore, these stories are not historical facts but rather myths made from 3rd and 4th hand rumors.

The great majority of historical opinions on Jesus were produced by Christians, who would "have faith" in him regardless of the facts. Regarding official documentation, there aren't any official Roman documents from the Levant during Jesus' lifetime. No official Roman document from the Levant during the time of Jesus exists, as far as official records are concerned. No military dispatches, no tax records, no trial records, no execution records, no census records, nothing. Not a single Roman document even mentions Pilate. Added to these are the Dead Sea Scrolls. Jesus is not mentioned in any of these works, which date from the second decade of the common era to the tenth decade. Following Constantine's adoption of Christianity as the official religion of the empire, the populace was faced with the severe ultimatum to either convert or die. After giving the command, Constantine distributed parts of the Bible to a number of scribes.

The time of Jesus as a purported living individual is not mentioned in secular history. According to the Bible, Jesus traveled around the countryside, performing miracles and speaking to crowds of people, but not a single headline was published. There was not a single letter from a witness to the miracles that described what they saw or that they could have written and passed on to another person. Josephus would have begun writing about the alleged crucifixion decades after it occurred, having been born in 37 AD. It wasn't until 116 AD that the Roman senator Tacitus wrote about the crucifixion.

Unusual Sequence of Evidence

1. The Synoptic gospels contradict one another by depicting a purported Jesus character that was not documented by anybody who really saw him in person, in addition to being written by anonymous authors a century after the events.
2. Neither the Apostles nor any eyewitnesses wrote the "gospels" in the story. Up to 130 years after Jesus' death, Mathew was written. The oldest, Mark, was written in 70 AD (40 years after Jesus's time), yet it still has no mention of miracle births, resurrections, or other such events. Jesus left no written legacy in modern history, neither his own works nor those of any contemporaries.
3. Epistles only speak of a pre-existent celestial being and revealed gospel.
4. A lifetime later, the gospels are wildly fictional. Not even the Gospels provide independent evidence.
5. No other evidence from the first 80 years of Christianity's growth has been preserved, not even in quote.
6. Tacitus and Josephus are cited by Christians, although neither of them saw him as the Son of God or as someone of great significance. Furthermore, the Testimonium Flavianum, the bigger of the Josephus stories, is generally believed to be a Christian bogus or interpolation. Josephus began writing about Jesus 6 decades after Jesus's lifetime. Additionally, Josephus was likely only retelling what he had heard, and at most, it was third hand. Josephus just recorded what others claimed; he had no direct knowledge of Jesus.
7. Tacitus was born twenty-five years after the supposed existence of Jesus. He did not claim to know Jesus directly and lived far too late to do so. Without offering any independent evidence, Tacitus just referred to and attested the myths and the cult's existence—not the man or god. In addition to not being an "eye witness," his "writings," including "The Annals," that make reference to Jesus are proven to be bogus.
8. There is no archaeological evidence of Jesus. Additionally, there is no tangible archaeological or physical proof that other religious figures like Jesus, Abraham, Isaac, Jacob, and Moses ever existed. There is very little evidence in the historical and archaeological record outside of biblical literature.

Why does everyone think Jesus is real, but Zeus is considered as mythology?

Currently, a lot of people believe in the story of Jesus; mythology is only recognised until a religion is extinct. Christianity would be identical to that of Ancient Greek mythology if everyone were to stop and reflect on it at some point. Given their tremendous wealth, power, and influence, which was obtained through Christian colonisers and militant organisations, this religion has been able to persist for a very long time. Rome did not take religion nearly as seriously unless it was being used for political purposes. One may claim that Zeus was not real, but Jesus was. However, given the facts, that cannot be accurate in the slightest. Nearly all of Jesus's characteristics are borrowed from earlier religions. I'm here to demonstrate these connections to you. So where is the origin of this story? First, let's talk about its name.

The Etymology Of Jesus Christ

The Hebrew form, which literally translates to "Joshua," is a little lengthier than the Aramaic form, which was Yeshu. Both would still be used, however, because they are only names and not the language itself. Furthermore, the common language was Aramaic, while biblical Hebrew was only used for reading the Scriptures in the synagogue. The universal language was Greek, and Jesus' name is spelled "Iēsoûs."

The name Jesus was "invented" by the English; prior to the 16th century, the letter "J" did not exist. The Latin "IESVS" changed to "Jesus." Jesus derives from the Greek word "Iesous," which means "Hail Zeus" or "Greetings Zeus" in Hebrew. An interesting connection is that the Bible was created and assembled by Greeks and Romans, who once perhaps worshipped the Greek Pantheon Zeus. Regarding the word "Christ", in the ancient Egyptian mythology, Horus was referred to as the messiah, the Gods' anointed, and "KRST" which was often found written upon mummies as a term meaning 'anointing' and 'blessing' from Horus. The Hebrew word "messiah" (anointed one) has its origins in the Egyptian word "messias," which is also used to refer to crocodiles. The term "Mashiach" (To Anoint) is created when vowels are added to the stem. Messiah, from the Greek word "christos," or "Christ," means "anointed one."

The upright mummy represented by the term "KRST" in Ancient Egypt is a metaphor for Christ's ascension. The name "Christ," "Christos" in Greek, "Christvs" in Latin, for the "anointed," comes from the Egyptian word "KRST."

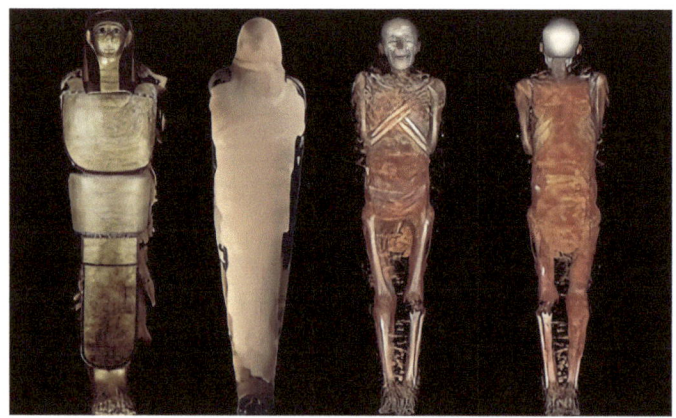

"Christianity derives from the English word 'Christ' which stems from the Greek word 'Christos' which means the anointed one. The Hebrew word 'Messiah' evolved from the Ancient Egyptian word 'Messias,' or 'MeSseH.' It refers to the crocodile god Sobek and crocodile fat.

The Hebrew term 'Messiah' in Greek is 'Christos,' coincidentally the appellation of Christos can be seen in our modern world 'Crisco' as in cooking oil. Anointing people with oil is a common occurrence in both new and old testaments. Why then a crocodile and its fat? Sobek's crocodile represented and stood for royal authority. It is associated with the Sun god Ra and the Sol of the Sun which is also represented by the crocodile. With connections to Zeus, Horus, Sobek, Saturn, and several other deities, Jesus Christ has been demonstrated to be nothing more than a recycled form of earlier gods. All of whom embody the solar characteristics of the Sun.

Sun = Son

The Sun has been the primary source and maintainer of Earthly life from the beginning of existence. Its powerful light drives out evil and purges sins. The Sun is the source and father of all living things, the creator and preserver, the saviour and redeemer. The Sun was the source of good in the world, driving away evil and allowing people to survive another day. It provides the source of power for everything that happens in our solar system. The Sun's original name was "O". "O" stands for Sun, and "On" is the same for "One". This term, which the Greeks created as "Helios" or "Sol," is thought to refer to the Sun. Consequently, we get the Greek God Helios, the guardian of oaths and the God of sight.

"O" was the true name of the Sun. As true theory tells us, this is the reason we turn "ON" our lights. The following will demonstrate the several ways the word "on" can be derived; they are Om, An, Am, Aun, Ani, or Ayin. In Sanskrit, Ani means "inside the Sun." It is on Ion, Aon, Aho, Ion, oni, On, Ono, and Oni in Greece, Egypt, and Palestine. The supreme god of Phoenicia, Elon, is a compound of El, the Sun, and appears as El, Aun, or Elion in Sanchoniathan's description of Phoenician gods. Eli and On, the names of the Sun, are combined to form the Canaanite phrase Eli-On.

Amun is derived from the ancient words amon, which means Sun. In the same way that the Sun god Aton was worshipped, the Sun was also called Abaddon, which the evangelist tells us was the same as Apollo or Apollon. The "Sun of man will arise with healing in his wings," according to Malachi. Thus, in Egypt, Messiah is compared to Apollo, El to the Sun. Thus, light is given by the Messiah (Sun God). The Sun, the combination of Phi, Ath, and On, was known by the ancient title Phaethon, a figure that is often misunderstood. Many people have a tendency to give vowels the nasal sound, which is the reason why there are so many names for the Sun that finish in "N" or are equivalent to "M".Thus, the Sun's original names became On, Un, An, Am, Om, and Um.

According to Jacob Bryant, Sun, San, and Zan are names of the Sun and have the same meaning. In Greek mythology, the tomb of Zeus of Crete, who was supposedly buried there, bore the following inscription; "Herein lies the great Zan (Sun), On now moving elegantly through the sky." The Sun was hence also known in Greek mythology as the "Eye of Zeus."

The Latin word solis, or Sun, was used to translate the Greek word Helios. The O, the Sun's first name, is the progenitor of all of them; even the Hel of Helios of the Greeks and the Al Adel of the Hebrews are only variations of sol or solas. Additionally, according to Jacob Bryant, the Egyptian priests were known as Sun Chin or Son Cohen, meaning priests of the Sun. Therefore, it is true to say that the Sun of God is the Son of God, and the English word for Sun is not a false cognate with Son. In actuality, practically every Sun God story from antiquity echoes the concept of being the Son of the Sun and the Sun God surrendering his only begotten Son. The words "sun" and "son," which are demonstrated to have the same meaning and definition at the core of their etymological roots, are therefore equivalent in a conventional sense.

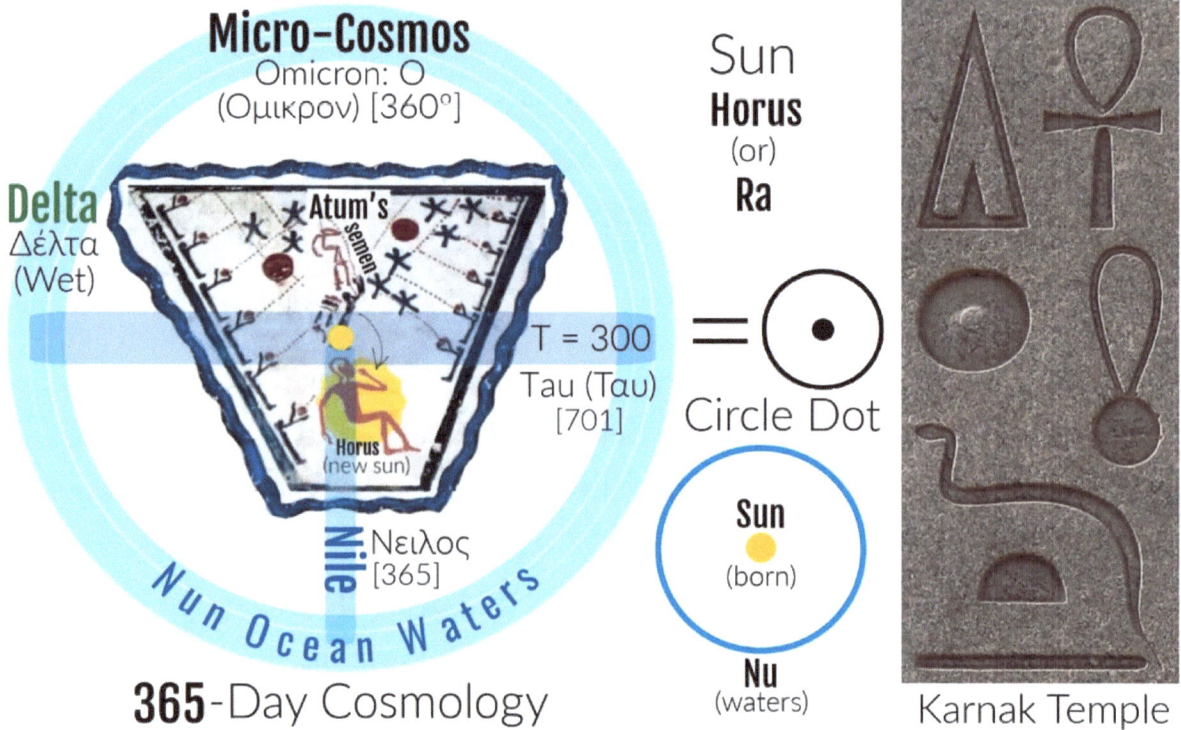

Egyptian Solar Circle Dot ☉ Symbol

Jesus of Nazareth Is The Sun of Mazzaroth

In the Old Testament, Josephus' writings, and early maps of the Holy Land, there is no such place as Nazareth. Furthermore, there is actually no documentation of Nazareth's existence at the time of Jesus. No book, map, chronicle, or military document from the era that has been uncovered to date mentions Nazareth. About thirty years after Jesus Christ's purported crucifixion, Nazareth emerged. During Jesus' early years, no one was from Nazareth. There was none. Neither the Talmud nor any early rabbinic literature mentions Nazareth, although naming sixty-three Galilean villages. In truth, the Nazarene sect's name came from an unexpected but well-known source. Mazzaroth, which means zodiac, is where it originated.

In theory, even if Nazareth had been in the distant past, the present-day site wouldn't fit into the description. The hill and synagogue where the elders would attempt to hurl Jesus were absent. Even now, there is no proof that Nazareth existed before the year 100 AD, including paved roads, signs for public buildings, or people. Only the existence of a single vineyard in the region is backed by evidence.

- **Luke 1:26** - "In the sixth month the angel Gabriel was sent by God to a town in Galilee called Nazareth"

- **Luke 2:39:** "So when they had performed all things according to the law of the Lord, they returned to Galilee, to their own city, Nazareth."

Mazzaroth (maz'-za-roth) is connected to the comparisons of the following word:
Mazzarah: (he resh zayin mem) m(ah) zz(aw)r(aw)h, maz-zaw-raw'; apparently from the heb. **NAZAR**, naw-zar', a primary root, to hold aloof, here specifically to set apart (to sacred purposes), I.E. Devote - consecrate, separate, thus used here in tee sense of distinction (only in the plural), perhaps collectively as the zodiac: Mazzaroth.

The root word for both Mazzaroth and Nazareth is the same. "A place up high you watch from or a place up high you look to" is what the word Nazareth (now en-Nasrah) means. However, in the

New Testament, it is associated with Netzer, which means "a branch." It should be clear that the true meaning of the name Jesus of Nazareth is the son of the zodiac or the constellations.

There is a fair amount of consensus that the constellations were creative works intended to tell stories. Through careful observation and documentation, ancient astronomers developed a high degree of prediction accuracy, such as during solar eclipses. Everybody who watched the night skies had become used to seeing the same groups of stars that filled the heavens. Month after month, these constellations moved across the sky, reappearing the next year in the same sequence. As a result, the idea that these star groups and movements could be used to document the vast cosmic story emerged. In fact, several stars and their constellations are mentioned by name in the Bible. In the book of Job, which is perhaps the oldest book in the Bible, this is especially so. The "sweet influences of Pleiades" (38:31), the "bands of Orion" (38:31), the "crooked Serpent" (26:13), "Arcturus with his sons" (38:32), and the "chambers of the south" (9:9) are all mentioned by Job.

Job 38:32, which asks, **"Canst thou bring forth Mazzaroth in his season?"** is arguably the most prominent passage relating to this topic. The term "mazzaroth" refers to the twelve signs of the zodiac and the constellations that go along with them, which is an important fact. The group of stars that are situated on the Sun's "ecliptic," or apparent path across the sky, during a certain month of the year is referred to by each sign. Naturally, these are constantly changing as the planet rotates around the Sun once a year. Knowing when to start a story is crucial since the Zodiac is meant to tell an account through the stars.

Jesus Christ Surrounded by the Zodiac Circle on the Roof of the Church in Dekoulou (or "Decoulou") Monastery of the 16th Century

Constellation Layout in Line With Biblical Scripture

Sign	Hebrew Meaning	Principle Stars	Decans
1. **Virgo** (virgin) associated with the tribe of *Zebulon*—the town of Nazareth is located on the border of Zebulon and Naphtali	Bethulah - The Promised Seed of the Woman (Gen. 3:15)	a. **Spica** (ear of corn) (in Hebrew, *Tsemech* (branch—same word used for the Messiah); Arabic, Al Zimach (the branch); Egypt, Aspolia (the seed); [see John 12:24] b. **Zavijava** (gloriously beautiful) e. **Al Mureddin** (who shall have dominion) [see Ps 72:8]; in Chaldee, Vindemiatrix (son who cometh)	**Coma** (The Desired) [Hag. 2:7] **Centaurus** (The Despised) [Isa. 53:3] **Bootes** (Coming One) [Rev. 14:14-16] includes *Arcturus* (He cometh) [Job 9:9], *Al Katurops* (treading underfoot), & *Nekka* (the pierced) [Zech. 12:10]
2. **Libra** (the scales or balance, weighing) associated with the tribe of *Levi*. {Arabic, Al Zubena (purchase, redemption); Coptic, Lambadia (station of redemption); Akkadian, Tulku (altar, sacred mound)}	Monzanaim - The balances—the price deficient balanced by the price which covers [see Ps 49:7 & 62:9]	a. **Zuben al Genubi** (Price deficient) b. **Zuben al Chemali** (Price which covers) [Rev. 5:9] c. **Zuben al Akrab** (Price of the conflict) (the star towards Centaurus & Victim Slain)	**The Crux** (the Cross) (in Hebrew, *Adom*—cut off (Dan 9:26)) **Lupus** (Victim or Victim Slain) (Heb. *Asedah* = to be slain; Egypt, *Sura* = a lamb) **Corona** (the Crown, Bestowed) (Heb. 2:9, Rev 5:9 Zech 9:16)
3. **Scorpio** (scorpion) associated with the tribe of *Dan*, but an eagle was used on the tribal standard rather than the scorpion	Akrab = scorpion, war, conflict Wounding him that cometh (Gen 3:13-16)	a. **Antares** (the wounding)	**Serpens** (trying to seize the crown) [Rev. 12] (the alpha star is *Alya* in Hebrew (accursed)) **Hercules** (right heel wounded, he who cometh, strong one) (the gamma star is *Ma'a syn* = sin offering)

4. **Sagittaurus** (the archer) associated with the tribe of *Ashur*	The archer, bow, conquering (Rev 6:2)		**Lyra** (the harp) (*Vega* is the alpha star = he shall be exalted (Rev 19:1); **Shelyh** (eagle) is the beta star) **Ara** (the altar) (Ps 21:9) **Draco** (the dragon, trodden on) (Ps 91:13 & Rev 12:9)
5. **Capricornus** (the Goat-Fish) associated with the tribe of *Naphtali*	The sin offering		**Sagitta** (the arrow) **Aquila** (the eagle) **Delphinus** (the dolphin)
6. **Aquarius** (the man, the water bearer) associated with *Reuben*	The Servant Man	*Scheat* (He who returneth)	**Piscis Australis** (the southern fish) **Pegasus** (the winged horse) contains **Markah** (returning from afar) **Cygnus** (the swan, Bird of Return) contains **Deneb** (the judge)
7. **Pisces** (The fishes) associated with *Simeon*	Dagin (the fishes) the fishes tied together; a divided kingdom		**Alrisha** (the Band that ties together) **Andromeda** (the Chained Woman) **Desma** (the Bound) **Cepheus** (the Crowned King) star names include "coming quickly" "redeemer" & "the breaker"
8. **Aries** (the Ram) associated with *Gad*	Taleh (the Lamb) [changed to a ram by the Romans] The Lamb Slain (John 1:29; Rev 5:9, 12)		**Cassiopeia** (the enthroned woman) in Hebrew - Schedir (the freed) **Cetus** (Sea Monster) **Perseus** (the Breaker)
9. **Taurus** (the Ox) associated with *Joseph*	Shur (the Ruler)		**Orion** (the hunter) in Hebrew means "the Dayspring"

			Eridanus (the River of the Judge)
			Auriga (the Shepherd)
10. **Gemini** (the Twins) associated with *Benjamin*	Thaumin (united)		**Lepus** (the hare) **Canis Major** (the big dog) in Hebrew: Zeeb (the wolf) **Canis Minor** (the little dog) in Hebrew - Lamb
11. **Cancer** (the Crab) associated with *Issachar*	Tegmine (the sheepfold) [representing the congregation of believers - re John 10]		**Ursa Major** (the greater sheepfold) alpha star is **Dubheh**, the herd. The Greeks mistook the sign of the herd for the sign of a bear. **Ursa Minor** (the lesser sheepfold) [there are 24 stars in these 2 decans circling the Pole Star (re Rev 4:4) **Argo** (the Ship) in Hebrew: Redeemed
12. **Leo** (the Lion) associated with *Judah*	Arieh (the Lion King)	**Regulus** (treading under foot) **Denebola** (the judge cometh) **Deneb Aleced** (the judge shall reign)	**Hydra** (the Fleeing Serpent) **Crater** (the Cup of Fire) **Corvus** (the Raven)

Chapter 2: Astrological Nature of the Bible

Astrological Nature of Jesus Christ

The thoughts and ideas of Christianity are not new; they are based on ancient mythology. It is simply paganism under a different name. Jesus's gospel is not a biography of a real-life Messiah. It is a pagan Jewish reimagining of common resurrecting gods that represent the Sun. It will be a somewhat painful, revelatory, and most importantly, beneficial experience to have old riddles solved and to make sense of our reality. However, as every nurse is aware, the scream method is the fastest way to pull a plaster off a wound. To deduce some of the amazing secrets that have been dumbing us down for years, however, we will require that. It takes two steps to reach sanity. You have to notice the darkness before you can reach the light. What we are discussing here, however, is the intellectual work that must now be completed in order to restore rationality to its rightful place.

"I have examined all the known superstitions of the world, and I do not find in our particular superstition of Christianity one redeeming feature. They are all alike, founded on fables and mythology. Millions of innocent men, women and children since the introduction of Christianity have been burned, tortured, fined and imprisoned. What has been the effect of this coercion? To make one half of the world fools and the other half hypocrites, to support roguery and error all over the Earth." **- Thomas Jefferson**

Virgo The Virgin and Sphinx

In contrast to us now, the Egyptians began their year in the sign of Virgo, which in those days, according to the processional movement of the heavens, was around July 20th or 25th. It was at this time that the Nile began to rise and the flood waters began to rise. During the season, which lasted from July 20 to July 25, Sirius, the star, was high in the sky. And it was when the Sun would rise into the Virgo sign or constellation. Naturally, Virgo is the sign of the virgin, who has long been portrayed as a woman, a goddess, a queen, or a stunning virgin who is Virgo. It goes without saying that if the Egyptians' year began in Virgo, then ours would also have twelve seasons and months to go until the year ends. In a symbolic sense, the female's head is meant to gaze out to the horizon. After tracing the entire Earth, her eyes return to the lion's body. All it is, is a zodiac sign. Standing 66 feet tall, it is a sandstone and zodiac sign. Leo is the final sign of the zodiac, whereas Virgo is the first and a sign of the virgin. When you combine them, you have the sphinx. The female, Virgo, was the one with the wheat sheaf in her hand. The Sun now moved into the Virgo sign on July 25th.

It was the notion that the Son of God was now being born in the symbol of a virgin or of a virgin in the stellar cult. When the Sphinx was built, its face was orientated with its eyes towards the horizon, even facing the area of the horizon where the constellations of Virgo and Leo rose at night. However, at night, Leo and Virgo would rise directly in front of the Sphinx's eyes. This zodiacal band was known as the girdle of Isis, the virgin goddess, because it started in Virgo. She was Mary's prototype. Horus was the son of Isis. Jesus was the son of Mary.

All things considered, the Christ myth was based on Horus, which his name means light or Sun. Thus that's where the term "horizon" or "zone of Horus" originates. Additionally, his name gives us "hours." Horus-Rising (Horizon), that's correct. That is the Sun's zone. Horus, the Sun god, is at the zone of the horizon as the Sun rises. In Shakespeare's day, "orisons" was the ancient name for prayers. As you say your horizons and prayers, you look east. What makes you look east? because that is where the Sun will rise. You worship the Sun. Solar culture is what it is.

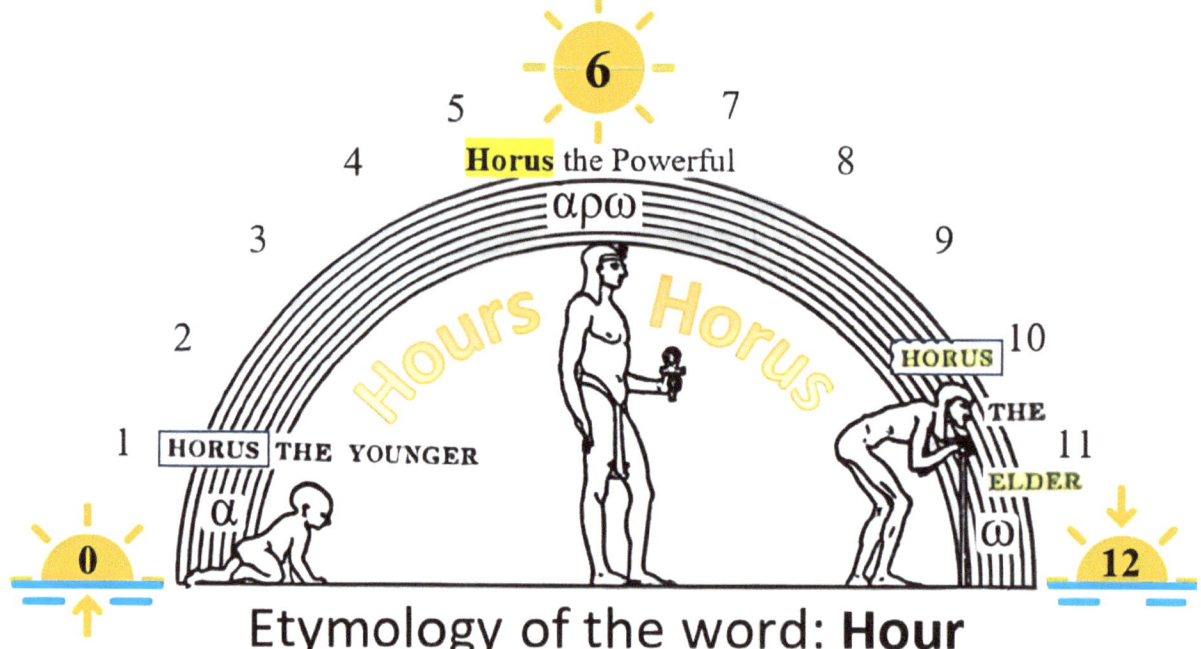

Once you have awakened your right brain, you merely need to examine the symbols. Your entire intellect is being used. You now know how to recognise patterns. You will discover that nothing is being hidden from you.

LEFT BRAIN FUNCTIONS	RIGHT BRAIN FUNCTIONS
uses logic	uses feeling
detail oriented	big picture oriented
facts rule	imagination rules
words and language	symbols and images
present and past	present and future
math and science	philosophy & religion
can comprehend	can "get it" (i.e. meaning)
knowing	believes
acknowledges	appreciates
order/pattern perception	spatial perception
knows object name	knows object function
reality based	fantasy based
forms strategies	presents possibilities
practical	impetuous
safe	risk taking

The divine spiritual spark that leads to greater thinking must first awaken the right brain. The "right brain" favors understanding why things happen, and if it is fully integrated with the left brain, it will be able to search for the truth and subjects beyond. For example we see the astrological motif in corporate logos today; Mother Mary with the crescent Moon beneath her feet and the Sun over her head. It is present in the present-day Columbia Pictures corporate logos. The Sun shining behind the back of the virgin. Or the one holding the huge torch, which in Virgo is the Sun.

Columbia Pictures Logo

This is taken advantage of by the solar cult, who then rearrange things. Horus's alignment with the Sun abruptly changes. Absolutely, but more in line with, for instance, Aries, Jesus holding God's lamb. The Sun, which is the sign of Aries, is universally recognised as the lamb or ram. As a result, they relocate the Son of God from Virgo to another place and identity. In earlier times, the bull and the cow God which symbolises Taurus, were worshipped.

Then the ram. The ram is a common symbol in Egypt as it represents Aries. The myths shift with the Sun. Therefore, the pyramid, the Sphinx, and numerous other tombs, temples, and other monuments are plainly astrological and astronomical. Additionally, you will see that the Sphinx has wings, claws, or scales even when you render or view it rendered. It has a lion's or dragon's tail, and a woman's head. Once more, that just symbolises the lion's body, wings, claws, and four corners coming together. The zodiac's cardinal points.

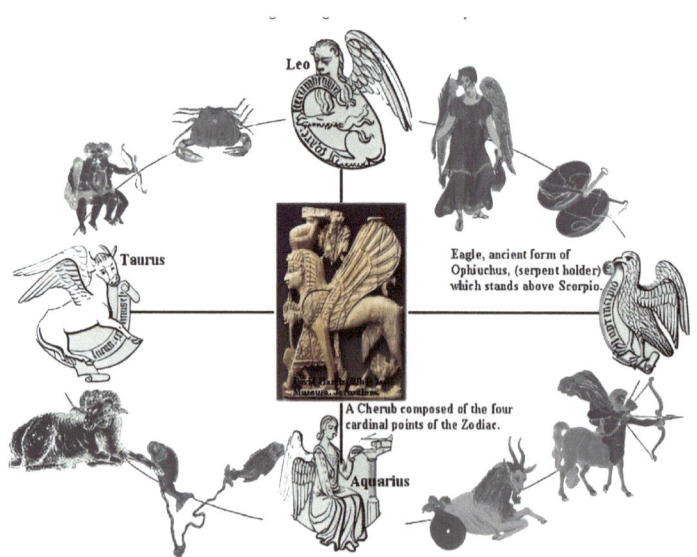

Christianity adopted elements of pagan belief systems, such as the cross, according to historical records. The purpose of its introduction was to promote the acceptance of "so-called Christianity". Originally used in an initiatory ceremony in ancient Egypt, the sign of the cross eventually made its way into Christianity. The Church asserts that it was not until far later than the sixth century that the cross was utilised in its history. The widespread use of the cross was authorised by the 6th Ecumenical Council in 680 AD. Emperor Hadrian I later authorised the new church symbol after the council decided to accept the image of a man tied to a cross. About a century later, the earliest depictions of Jesus Christ standing against a cross start to appear. As a result, the cross abruptly enters the discussion 800 years after Christianity was founded.

The cross has been used for aeons in the ancient world and is not exclusive to Christianity. Once more, the zodiac is its source. Astronomy and astrology would not be possible without two additional significant cycles and events in the skies. These are referred to as the celestial equator and the ecliptic. The main constellations are situated in a band that is around 17 degrees wide and represents the Sun's orbit around the Earth. It is the zodiac. Currently, this belt crosses the celestial equator, another belt. The spring and fall equinoxes occur each year as the Sun reaches the intersection of this cross. The spring and fall equinoxes occur when the Sun crosses the ecliptic and celestial equator, which is where those two come together.

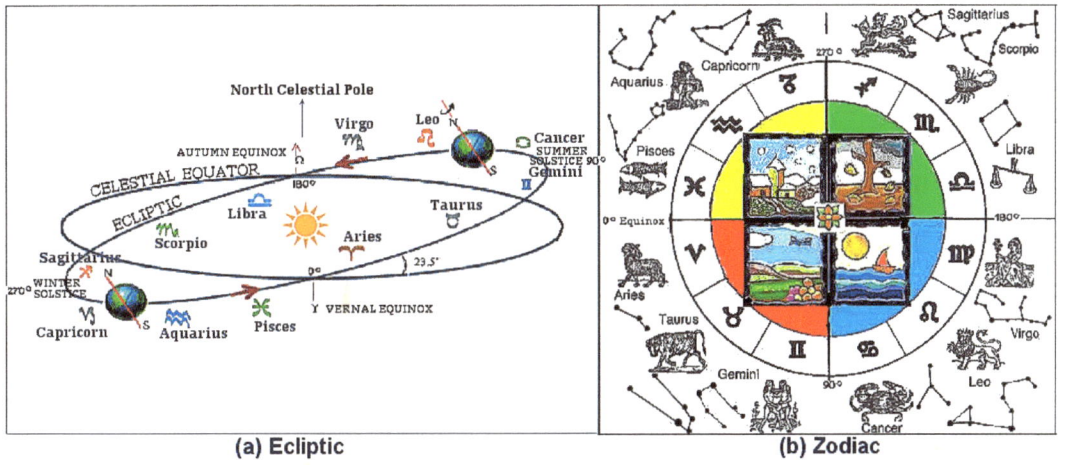

(a) Ecliptic (b) Zodiac

As you can see in this diagram, the solstices and equinoxes occur at the connecting points of the two belts as the Sun moves closer to those two junctions. Naturally, there are two of each, for a total of four.

Since John realised that the 12 disciples and Jesus, who had been the Sun from the time of his nativity, were all part of the solar worship, he used that initial cross as the emblem of Christianity. Additionally, he wanted the cross to stand in for the great cross of the zodiac, often known as the zodiacal cross. How many flags do you know in the world that contain that cross? There are, in fact, many. Naturally, though, they are concentrating on the crossing point of the equator and the ecliptic. So, when you hear Christians calling out and discussing how they followed Christ to the crucifixion, simply recognise what the cross is.

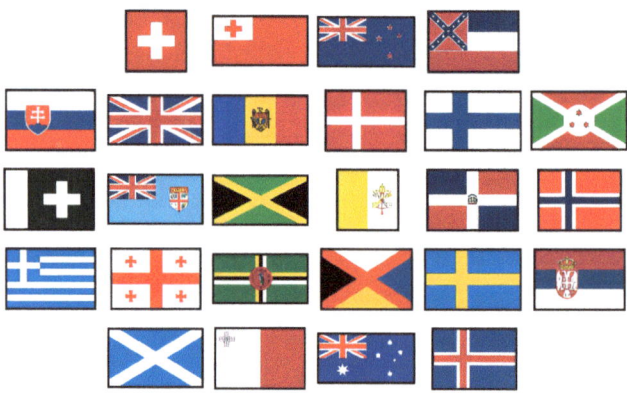

When you hear about Jesus' death on the cross, you should know that it is the winter cross, and that he is dying there in order to be reborn three days later.

- **Luke 23:47 -** Now when the centurion saw what had taken place, he praised God, saying, "Certainly this man was innocent!"

Centurion is a cryptic message that refers to the warrior Aries. As the Sun is fading (dying), the centurion notices what is going on in the Aries. Despite his innocence, he realises that God is fading (dying).

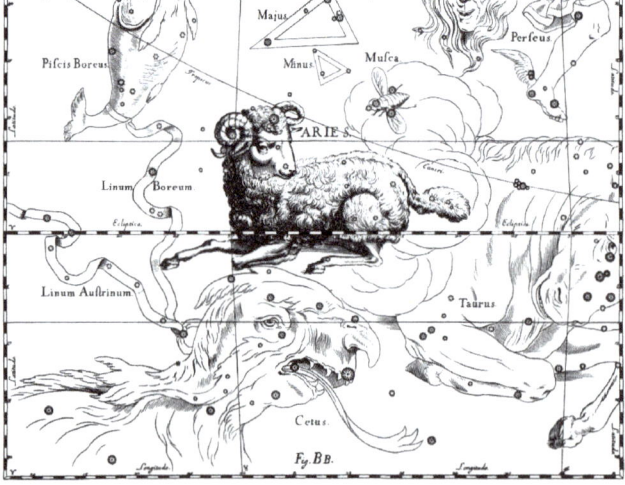

Dying On The Cross of Winter

Additionally, the southern signs are referenced by Jesus' burial in the cave or tomb, when the Sun falls into the dark signs of winter. It simply represents entombment. This is found in Lazarus's story. This is found in Osiris's story. Additionally, all of the world's Christ-saviors enter the dark realm for a temporary stay before returning. Christ also declared that he will rise again on the third day. From Capricorn to Aries, the third day can be viewed as the three signs. Capricorn, Aquarius, and Pisces are the three signs that span from the depths of winter to spring. Three days, three seasons, and three time periods come to mind. Now that we have examined the birth of Jesus, we also hear a very precise detail.

At age 33, Christ passes away. The answer to that is, once more, related to the equinoxes' precession. In about one month of thirty days, the Sun crosses three degrees across each sign of the zodiac as it goes backwards through the zodiac. At the first degree, it enters a sign, and by the thirty-third degree, it is entirely out of the sign. Jesus, the Son of God, was claimed to have died at the age of 33 for this reason. It also explains why Masonry has 33 degrees. The Stellar Cult is the primordial lineage of Freemasons.

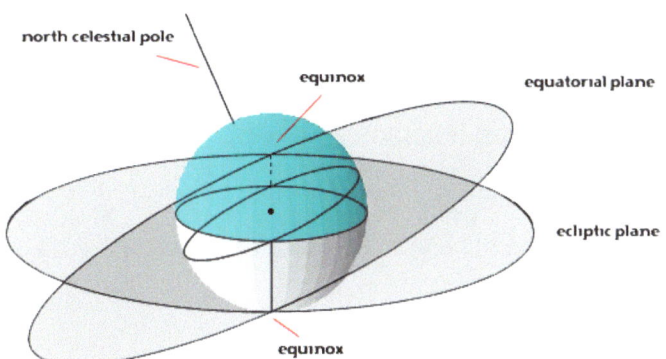

33 Vertebrates - Christ Consciousness

The 33 vertebrae in the human body symbolise a person's spiritual path; it is a master number that signifies Christ consciousness. Many spiritual traditions believe that Kundalini energy, a primal power that resides at the base of our spine, may be awakened and ascended through the spine. This energy signifies great transformation and spiritual enlightenment as it ascends through the vertebrae and approaches the crown chakra. A metaphor for the turning point in spiritual symbolism, Jesus Christ's crucifixion at the age of 33 symbolises the fulfilment of a divine purpose and the height of enlightenment. The turning point in spiritual symbolism is symbolised by Jesus Christ's crucifixion at the age of 33, which signifies the fulfilment of a divine mission and the height of enlightenment.

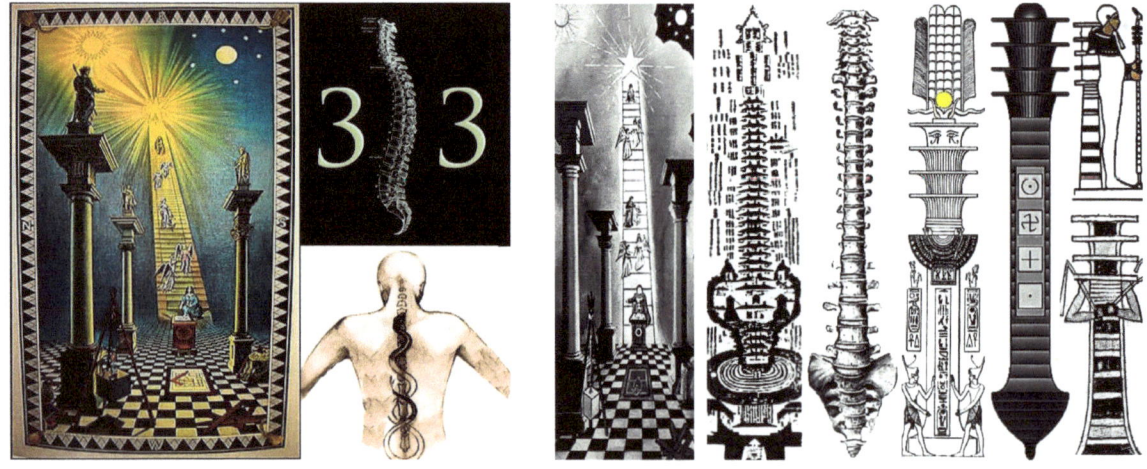

Our Father Who Art In Heaven

As stated in the Father Prayer, Jesus refers to himself as "Our Father, who art in heaven" in reference to the Sun, Venus, and morning star. A sign is 30 degrees above the Sun, which is 3 degrees. It's around thirty degrees to travel thirty degrees, but it's roughly thirty-three degrees to leave it altogether. Once more, the references can be found in the Bible. "I am the root and offspring of David and the bright and morning star," Jesus declares in Revelation 22:16, "I'm the bright and morning star." You are not allowed to worship it, speak about it, or use astrology. All of it is supposed to be forbidden, evil, and Satanic. However, it is okay for Jesus to say that he identifies with the heavens and the stars. That is ironic, isn't it? The morning star is Venus or the Sun.

Jesus of Nazareth

No place called Nazareth existed. The word comes from the Egyptian words Nasir, which means Sirius, and Nazir, which means "Prince who is sent." Jesus of Na-Sirius is the one (alluding to the zodiac). Additionally, the name "carpenter" is derived from the word "naggar," which means serpent-priest. These kinds of cover euphemisms are still used by Freemasons today in place of the word "mason." Even though they use the word "carpenter," everyone in the know is aware of what it means. We should also know that the Sun god falls into the feminine signs. The notion was that the son is born in the virgin, dies, and returns to the mother, which is the night sky, eternally, despite the fact that Christians put a lot of effort into dismissing it.

A biography is not what the Gospels are. A sidereal fiction, the Bible was and still is nothing more than an astrological tale. The authors of the Bible, in my opinion, were aware that they would never present it at any other event. Furthermore, they would have been shocked that people today would genuinely believe it to be a biography. The endeavour to include basic evidence to support a physical presence in relation to biblical stories must have been done far better. If it were real, the writers would have already addressed many of the queries we posed in order to verify the Bible since they would be the ones bearing the burden. However, the ancient allegorists were aware that everyone was aware that this was simply a fable. This is verified by the fact that the scriptures will start to disclose their hidden meanings if the terms zodiac and constellations are used in place of the following ones. Which terms? Take as many as you like. Bethlehem, Nazareth, New Jerusalem, and the Tabernacle. Aeons or Ages, seasons, oracles, the Hall of Judges, the Kingdom of God, the Tent of God, and Flocks at Night, Citadel, The Mount of Olives, the Mount of Glory, the City of David, Heaven, the Celestial City, the Throne of the Elect, the Seven Churches, The Most High's Home, The Mercy Seat, and the most sacred location, the Labyrinth, are all here. Instead, use the words constellations of the zodiac and observe what occurs whenever you come across these odd, enigmatic, and untranslatable concepts in the Bible. You may be surprised.

Originally, the patriarchs—Abraham, Jacob, Moses, Solomon, David, Samson, Joseph, Daniel, Jesus, and all the others—represented conjunctions and alignments between the planets and the stars. Their many wives, children, and daughters are only zodiacal arc degrees and minutes.

- Although Samson was the son, God is the Sun. Actually, the term "shamash" means "Samson." The word "shamash" in Hebrew means "Sun."
- In the lion's den, Daniel either fought the lions or was rescued from them. Based on the Son of God, the entire concept is that Leo is going through the hardships of the sign because, like Hercules, if you're the hero, you have to go through the 12 signs.
- Now, the Bible contains the identical phrase we use, "Amen, Amen," which is the word of God. We say "Amen" at the conclusion of a prayer. According to the Egyptian pantheon, Amen is actually Amen Ra.
- Adonai, the god of the Hebrews, is descended from Aton, the solar god. In Egyptian, the T turns into a D. In Egyptian, Amon, who art in heaven, is the prayer that reveals Amon.
- Lazarus originated from La Asuras, an Egyptian. The Indian Surya, which also represents the Sun, is Asura. However, Osiris's previous name actually was Asurya. They referred to him as Asurya, the Sun, rather than Osiris. The Sun, Surya, belongs to the Indians. Lazarus emerges, mummy-wrapped, out of the dark tomb.

If the word Sun (S U N) is substituted with the word Son (S O N) whenever the former appears in the Bible, it will be evident that every single text fits the real Sun and not a man. The verses really make more sense. Put the word Sun there and think of the Sun whenever you see the words "Son of God" or "Jesus" in your head, and the Bible will spring to life.

- According to Revelation 1:7, "Behold, he cometh with clouds." Indeed, clouds surround the Sun. Even today, churches and Christians raise their arms and display the ancient Ka sign. If you open any Egyptian mythology book, you will notice the Ka, or the gods extending their arms. In order to represent the soul, lift your arms in such a manner. On the most basic level, however, simply look at the artwork. Just take a look at the images that are being shown to you—Christ, surrounded by light. Amen, which literally translates to "the Sun God," is how we conclude our prayers. "Our Father who art in heaven."

9th Century, Zodiac Christ | Christ as associated with the Sun God, The Father.

- Jesus states, "I am the root and offspring of David and the bright and morning star," in Revelation 22:16. Jesus is referred to as the Most High at the age of twelve. He is called the Most High in the Bible. The Sun is at its highest point when it is at noon, which is twelve o'clock. Christ is derived from the Egyptian KRST, which means made flesh, as previously said. Therefore, the term "ancient" is derived from the word "KRST," which means "to be made flesh." As a secondary meaning, it also implies to be anointed with oil. Christ is believed to be the one who is baptised or oiled.
- It was the tradition of the heathens to celebrate the Sun's birthday on December 25th by igniting lights as a sign of celebration. The Christians participated in these celebrations and solemnities as well. As a result, the Church decided that the actual Nativity should be solemnised on that day and the Epiphany feast on January 6th after seeing that Christians had a preference for this celebration. Consequently, in addition to this tradition, the fire-kindling traditions persisted until the sixth.

The purpose of the Bible is to give you the impression that God is wrathful and up in the clouds. In addition, you have a strict father figure who judges everything you do in an attempt to make you so schizoid, pathological, and existentially deranged that you are unable to even control your own thoughts or destiny. The Christian mind is exposed to the concern of a psychological influence that has been nothing short than severe insanity, causing a trauma to the mind that has caused sickness and, to some extent, destroyed the natural desires for happiness. However, this entire onslaught on the human psyche was intended to do that. To keep the starvation from spreading and to detach you from the Earth. It is all about having that imaginary friend that children have and that comforts them. It is the unspoken desire to have a parent, guardian, ideal friend, a celestial dictatorship.

The SON of God Is the Sun

There are many carvings and writings of the Sun dating back to 10,000 BC that demonstrate people's reverence and devotion for this star. It is easy to see why the Sun rises every morning, providing warmth, sight, and security while shielding humanity from the cold, blindness, and predator-filled darkness of the night. The cultures realised that without it, life on Earth would cease to exist and the crops would not flourish. The Sun became the most beloved creation of all time because of these realities. They also had a keen awareness of the stars. Through the tracking of the stars, they were able to identify and predict long-term occurrences like eclipses and full moons.

In the past, astronomy and astrology were actually one combined science. Astronomy was important because it was believed that a living entity or life force propelled the planets. For this reason, integrating astrology with astronomy was highly valued by the Chaldeans, Greeks, and Romans. Dendera, for instance, shows this by displaying an ancient zodiac. Ironically, however, the zodiac—which is made up of the twelve signs—appears about 500 BC, at the same time that the Old Testament scriptures were edited. Astrology predates the Bible by approximately 1300 years.

One of the first conceptual symbols in human history is the cross of the zodiac. Over the course of a year, it represents the Sun as it metaphorically moves through the 12 major constellations. In addition, it represents the four seasons, the solstices, equinoxes, and the 12 months of the year. The term "Zodiac" references the personification of celestial constellations in the form of animals or figures. In other words, the early civilizations did not only follow the Sun and stars, they personified them with extensive myths involving their movements and relationships. The

Sun was personified as a symbol of the invisible creator or God, God's Sun, the world's light, and humanity's saviour because of its life-giving and saving qualities.

In a similar way, the Sun's experiences were symbolised by the twelve constellations, which were named after natural occurrences that occurred throughout the time period. Aquarius, for instance, is the water-bearer who brings the spring rains. Horus was Egypt's Sun God about 3000 BC. His life is a sequence of allegorical myths about the Sun's movement in the sky, and he is the Sun anthropomorphised. We have a lot of knowledge on this solar messiah from the ancient Egyptian hieroglyphics. For example, Horus, who represented the Sun or light, had an enemy named Set, who represented the night or darkness. In metaphorical terms, Horus would defeat Set every morning, but Set would defeat Horus and cast him into the underworld every evening. It's important to remember that good vs evil, or dark versus light, is one of the most common mythical pairs ever and is still represented on a number of levels today.

Battles Between Horus and Seth - Edfu Temple

In general, there are many saviours from many periods and regions around the world who have these common characteristics. Why these qualities exist is still a mystery. What prompted the December 25th virgin birth? Why the inevitable resurrection after three days of death? Why were there 12 followers or disciples?

The virgin Mary gave birth to Jesus Christ in Bethlehem on December 25. Three kings or magi followed the star in the east that announced his birth in order to find and worship the new Saviour. Jesus was a child teacher at 12. He started his ministry at the age of 30 after being baptised by John the Baptist. Jesus travelled about with his 12 disciples, performing miracles like walking on water, curing the sick, and resurrecting the dead. In addition, Jesus was referred to as the Lamb of God, the Alpha and Omega, the Light of the World, the King of Kings, the Son of God, and countless more names. Following his betrayal by his disciple Judas, Jesus was sold for 30 pieces of silver, crucified, and buried. Three days later, he rose from the dead and ascended into heaven. The birth sequence is entirely astrological, to start.

Sirius, the brightest star in the night sky, is the one in the east. On December 24, it will line up with the three brightest stars in Orion's Belt. These three brilliant stars in the Belt of Orion are known today as the Three Kings, as they were in antiquity. On December 25th, the position of the sunrise can be seen by the Three Kings and Sirius, the brightest star. For this reason, the three kings follow the sunrise by following the eastern star. The Sun's birth Virgo, also referred to as Virgo the Virgin, is the constellation that represents the Virgin Mary. Another name for Virgo is the House of Bread. Additionally, a virgin carrying a sheaf of wheat is the symbol for Virgo; the house of silver and bread.

The harvest months of August and September are symbolised by the house of bread and its wheat symbol. Conversely, the literal translation of Bethlehem is "house of bread." Therefore, Bethlehem refers to the constellation Virgo, which is a place in the sky rather than on Earth. Around December 25, or the winter solstice, there is another fascinating phenomenon. The days get colder and shorter from the summer solstice to the winter solstice. Additionally, the Sun appears to migrate southward and become smaller and more scarce from the Northern Hemisphere's point of view.

To the ancients, the process of death was symbolised by the shortening of the days and the expiry of the harvests as the winter solstice drew closer. It was the Sun's death. And the Sun's death was over by December 22. When the Sun reaches its lowest position in the sky after six months of continuous southward movement. A fascinating event happens here. For three days, the Sun pauses going south, at least as far as can be seen. Additionally, the Sun sits close to the Southern Cross, also known as the Crux or Australis constellation, during this three-day break. The Sun then moves one degree to the north on December 25th, portending longer days, warmth, and spring. According to this story, the Son died on the cross, laid in death for three days, and then resurrected from the dead. For this reason, the concept of Jesus' crucifixion, three-day death, and resurrection is shared by many other Sun gods. It is the time before the Sun changes course and returns to the Northern Hemisphere, bringing along its spring and, with it, salvation. But it wasn't until Easter or the spring equinox that they celebrated the Sun's resurrection. This is because the Sun formally defeats the evil darkness during the spring equinox, and the rejuvenating conditions of spring emerge when the daytime extends beyond the night.

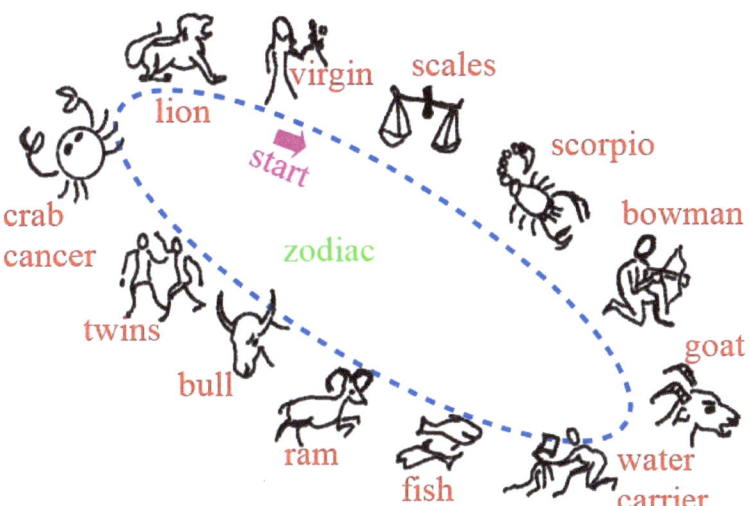

Scorpio The Back Biter

Notably, Judas is the backbiter or Scorpio in the cosmic mythology, denoting the season when the Sun is at its weakest. The scorpion stings Horus in the Egyptian version. In other words, the winter cold reduces the Sun's heat. Moreover, the lunisolar mythology also relates to Judas's betrayal of Jesus for thirty pieces of silver. The thirty silver pieces represent the Moon's cycle period or the 30 days of lunation. In the Gospel story, Jesus is also hung on a cross and stabbed in the side with a spear. A common practice in Sun God mythology is the side wounding of the sacred king victim. This practice also symbolises the Sun's yearly weakening in the sign of Sagittarius, the archer, as the winter solstice draws near.

The twelve disciples are perhaps the most evident example of the astrological symbolism surrounding Jesus. They are only the twelve Zodiac constellations that Jesus, as the Sun, moves around in. In fact, the Bible uses the number 12 a lot. Returning to the Zodiac's cross, the Sun's symbol of life, this was more than only a means of tracking the trajectory of the Sun or an artistic expression. Additionally, it was a pagan spiritual symbol, with this shorthand.

Zodiacal Cross and Jesus

This is a pagan-inspired version of the Zodiac cross, not a Christian symbol. Jesus is always depicted with his head on the cross in early occult art because of this. Jesus is the Son of God, the light of the world, the Risen Saviour who will return as it does each morning, and the glory of God who protects against the works of evil because he is born again every morning and appears in the clouds, up in heaven with his crown of thorns, or in the Sun rays.

- "As long as I am in the world I am the light of the world" - John 2:5
- "And go quickly, and tell his disciples that he is risen from the dead" - Matthew 28:6
- "And if I go and prepare a place for you, I will come again, and receive you" - John 14:2
- "To give the light of knowledge of the glory of God" - 2 Cor 4:6-15
- "Let us cast off the works of darkness and let us put on the armor of light" - Romans 13:12
- "Verily, I say unto thee, except a man be born again, he cannot see the kingdom" - John 3:3
- "They shall see the SON coming in the clouds" - Mark 13:26
- "But he came down from heaven." - John 6:38
- "Even the son which is in heaven" - John 3:13
- "Then came jesus forth, wearing a crown of thorns" - John 19:5

The Ages - Biblical Astrotheology

Now, one of the most significant astrological and astronomical analogies in the Bible is related to the ages. The age is mentioned several times in the Scriptures. We must be aware of the precession of the equinoxes in order to fully understand this phenomenon. The ancient Egyptians and many other cultures realised that sunrise on the morning of the spring equinox would fall at a different sign of the zodiac roughly every 2150 years. This is related to the Earth's gradual angular wobble while it revolves on its axis. Because the constellations move backwards instead of during their usual annual cycle, it is known as a precession. It will take the procession about 25,765 years to pass past all 12 signs. Ancient cultures were well aware that this year was also known as the Great Year.

The Ages - Scriptures

- "I am with you always to the very end of the age" - Matthew 28:20
- "Either in this age or the age to come" - Matthew 12:32
- "The harvest is the end of the age" - Matthew 13:39
- "Sign of your coming and the end of the age" - Matthew 24:3
- "In this age and the age to come" - Luke 18:30
- "Wise by the standards of this age" - Corinthians 3
- "On whom the fulfillment of the Ages has come" - Corinthians 10
- "Not only in the present age but the age to come" - Ephesians 1
- "In order that in the coming ages" - Ephesians 2:7-9
- "And the powers of the coming age" - Hebrews 6:5
- "He has appeared once and for all at the end of the ages" - Hebrews 9:26
- "King of the ages" - Revelation 15:3
- "Of the former age" - Job 8:8

Every 2150 years was referred to as an age by them. Taurus the Bull lived between 4300 and 2150 BC. The period of Aries the ram's life was 2150 BC to 1 AD. And the era of Pisces lasted from 1 AD to 2150 AD. Additionally, the next age of Aquarius will begin around 2150. In general, the Bible shows a metaphorical progression through three ages. When Moses brings the Ten Commandments down Mount Sinai, he is furious to find his people worshipping a golden bull calf, foreshadowing a fourth in the Old Testament.

Moses told his people to murder one another to cleanse themselves after shattering the stone tablets. The majority of biblical scholars would explain this rage by pointing out that the Israelites were worshipping a false idol or something similar. In actuality, Taurus the bull is the golden bull. And Aries the Ram's new age is symbolised by Moses. Jews continue to blast the ram's horn because of this. Moses is a symbol of the Aries' new age. And everyone must let go of their old age and enter a new one. These shifts are also marked by other gods, such as Mithra, a pre-Christian deity who uses the same symbolism to slaughter the bull.

The era of Pisces, the age of the two fish, or the period after Aries is now ushered in by Jesus. The New Testament has several instances of fish symbolism. Jesus uses bread and two fish to feed 5,000 people. He makes friends with two fishermen who join him as he starts his mission by walking around Galilee. We've all probably seen the Jesus fish on the backs of cars. They have no idea what it truly means. The Catholic Church also reinstates this, with the popes donning the Fish God, Dagon's mitre, on their heads.

In the age of Pisces, it is a pagan astrological symbol representing the Sun's kingdom. Furthermore, Jesus believed that the day of his birth marked the beginning of this age. Jesus is questioned by his followers about the location of the last Passover in Luke 22:10. Jesus said, "Behold, when ye are entered into the city, there shall a man meet you bearing a pitcher of water. Follow him into the house where he enters." Of all the astrological references, this scripture by far is the most revealing. Aquarius, the water carrier, is represented by the man holding the pitcher of water. He often appears as a man pouring out a pitcher of water. He represents the post-Pisces age.

Age of Aquarius

Additionally, as Aquarius follows Pisces in the equinoxes precession, Jesus will enter the house of Aquarius when the Son of God leaves the age of Pisces. Jesus simply says that the age of Aquarius will follow the age of Pisces. All of us have heard about the end of the world and the end of the times. A major basis of this concept, notwithstanding the Book of Revelation's whimsical depictions, is Matthew 28:20, where Jesus states, "I will be with you even to the end of the world." The word "world" is one of several mistranslations in the King James edition, however. The word in question is really aeon, which suggests age. Matthew 28:20 "I will be with you even to the end of the age." This is true as the Sun's transition into the age of Aquarius will mark the end of Jesus' solar entering personification. All of the concepts about the end of the world and the end of the times are misconstrued astrological allegories.

As a literary and astrological mixture, the character of Jesus is essentially a plagiarization of the Egyptian Sun god Horus. For example, images of the annunciation, the miraculous birth, and the worship of Horus were inscribed on the walls of the temple of Luxor in Egypt around 305 BC. Thoth informs the virgin Isis that she will become pregnant with Horus at the start of the images. Neph, the Holy Ghost, then impregnates the virgin, followed by the virgin's birth and adoration. This is precisely how Jesus' miraculous conception came to be. The literary parallels between the Christian and Egyptian religions are rather astounding. With more than 200 cited assertions across different eras and civilisations, the idea of a catastrophic flood permeates the ancient world. The Epic of Gilgamesh, which was written around 2600 BC, is a pre-Christian source, though, and one need not search much beyond. The story describes a massive flood that God ordered, an ark that held rescued animals, and even the release and reappearance of a dove. Among many other things, they were all identical to the biblical account. Then there is the Moses story, which has been plagiarised.

The Bible copied it's flood origin story from the Epic of Gilgamesh. The Story of Gilgamesh predates the Bible by over 1000 years.

According to legend, Moses escaped infanticide by being born in a reed basket and abandoned in a river. Later, a daughter of royalty saved him and brought him up as a prince. The myth of Sargon of Akkad was the primary source of this child in a basket story. Sargon was born in 2250 BC, adrift on a river, and placed in a reed basket to prevent infanticide. Akki, a royal midwife, then saved him and raised him.

Sargon's Birth: Placed in a basket set adrift in a river to avoid infanticide rescued and raised by royalty

In addition, Moses is regarded as the Lawgiver, the Mosaic Law, and the Giver of the Ten Commandments. Yet another ancient theme is the concept that God gave a prophet a law when he was on a mountain. There are many lawgivers throughout renowned history, and Moses is only another one. Manu was considered the greatest lawgiver in India. Zeus bestowed the holy rules upon Minos as he climbed Mount Dikta in Crete. The rules of God were inscribed on stone tablets that Mises held when he was in Egypt. Menu: Moses, Mises, and Menos. The Ten Commandments are also directly extracted from the Egyptian Book of Dead's spell 125. These terms were taken from the Book of the Dead; "I have not stolen" became "Thou shall not steal," "I have not killed" became "Thou shall not kill," "I have not told lies" became "Thou shall not bear false witness," and so on. These terms were taken from the Book of the Dead. In fact, the Judeo-Christian theology most likely has its start in the Egyptian religion. Egyptian beliefs predate Christianity and Judaism by a long way. These beliefs include the Great Flood, Easter, Christmas, Passover, saviours, the Ark of the government, baptism, the afterlife, the final judgement, virgin birth, death and resurrection, crucifixion (impaling), and many more.

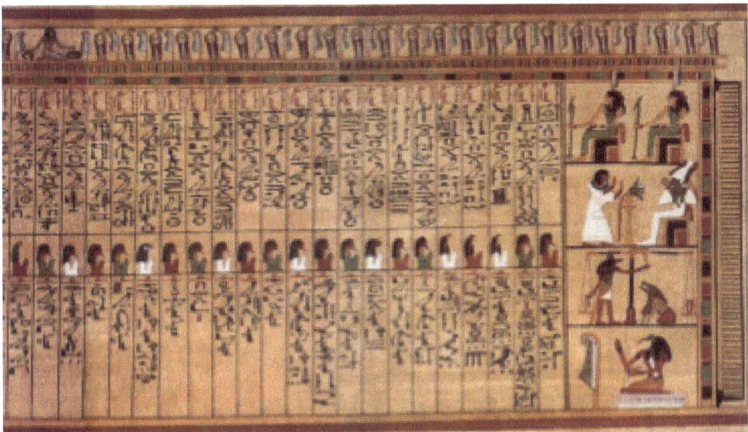

The Ten Commandments are directly extracted from the Egyptian Book of Dead's spell 125 - Over 1,500-years before Christian times

Like almost all religious stories before it, the Bible is really a literary combination of astrology and theology. In actuality, the story itself contains examples of the transference of one character's characteristics to another. The story of Joseph is found in the Old Testament. Jesus was modelled after Joseph. Joseph was father's favorite. Jesus was father's favorite. Joseph was a shepherd. Jesus was called the "Good Shepherd". Joseph was raised in the Promised Land. Jesus was raised in the Promised Land. Joseph was sold for 20 pieces of silver. Jesus was sold for 30 pieces of silver. Joseph's brothers disbelieved in him. Jesus's brothers disbelieved in him. Joseph's brothers casted him into a pit. Jesus was casted into a pit. The parallels are endless.

In addition, is there any historical proof that someone other than Jesus Christ, the son of Mary, ever lived and travelled with 12 disciples, healed people, and so on? Many historians were present in the Mediterranean region during or just after Jesus' supposed existence. What percentage of these historians record this number? Not one. To be fair, though, that doesn't imply those who support the historical Jesus haven't made the opposite argument. Four historians are usually used to support the existence of Jesus. The first three are Suetonius, Tacitus, and Pliny the Younger. Their records are at most just a few sentences long and only mention Christus or the Christ, which is actually a title rather than a person. The anointed one, that is. For hundreds of years, it has been established that Josephus, the fourth source, is a forgery. Unfortunately, it is nonetheless taken as truth. You would assume that a man who rose from the dead and ascended into heaven would have been documented in history so that everyone can see and witness the multitude of miracles that were attributed to him.

The Terms "Holy" and "Bible" Are Synonymous With "Sun Book."

The term "holy" is just a sarcastic utterance of the Phoenician word "heli," which is the root of the Greek word "helio helios," which means "the Sun." The term Bible, which was originally a diminutive of biblos, which means papyrus scroll of Semitic origin, was borrowed into Middle English via Old French from the ecclesiastical Latin 'biblia", which was derived from Greek 'biblia" books from 'Biblian books". Thus, the Holy Bible equals 'Sun Book", and 'Heli-biblos" equals 'Helios-Biblia".

We discover that Christianity was actually just a political development of a Roman myth. As the Sun deity of the Gnostic Christian sect, Jesus was actually a fictitious person, much like all previous pagan gods. For the sake of societal control, the political elite attempted to historicise Jesus. Emperor Constantine convened the Council of Nicaea in Rome in 325 AD. The politically driven Christian doctrines were developed during this assembly. In other words, started a lengthy history of spiritual deception and religious violence. The Vatican afterwards continued to exert political control over all of Europe for the following 1,000 years. In addition to enlightening events like the Inquisition and the Crusades, Christianity is a historical fraud, along with all other similar theologies. Nowadays, these religions are used to separate humanity from nature and from one another. They advocate obediently accepting authority. As a result, awful crimes can be justified under the pretext of a heavenly effort, reducing human accountability to the point where God governs everything. The political elite, who have been utilising the myth to dominate and influence societies, are most significantly strengthened by it. The religious myth, the most potent tool ever invented, provides the psychological foundation for the growth of other myths.

The Numerology of Jesus Christ

As previously said, the Bible itself is filled with secret meanings and codes, many of which are revealed through numerology, an ancient type of cypher. The study of Hebrew or Greek letter numbers as they relate to biblical interpretation is known as gematria, or biblical numerology. In gematria, each numerical number has significance and meaning. It is calculated by combining words and letters to represent a particular number associated with its meaning.

The Bible itself offers a multitude of numerological concepts and places a strong focus on certain numbers, such as "666," "33," "3," "12," "7," and so on. This will enable us to have a deeper comprehension of many of the esoteric elements revealed in the Bible through decoding.

The Solar Principle of 666

The solar numerals 6666 and 666, as well as 66, 6, 660, and 60, all refer to the circle and its sixfold geometry. Allah's numerical equivalent in Islamic numerology is 66. The hexagram or six-pointed star is known as the Seal of Solomon in Judaism. It may be found in all Freemasonry branches. Since the book of Revelation mentions the number of those who abuse power and authority, the number 666 becomes notorious in the west. However, 666 is more commonly associated with the Sun. Additionally, it is a number of Christ. The force that brings order to the chaos on Earth is the Sun 666 blazing from above. Only if this power is misused will it lead to abuse. The author of Revelation associated the Antichrist or the Beast with this unstable expression of 666. This is the reason why 666 has been associated with ideas of extreme negativity or the devil. However, this was not what it originally meant.

Six protons, six neutrons, and six electrons make up carbon 12, the most prevalent carbon isotope and the building block of all known life on Earth. The solar number 666 is reflected in the three 60-degree angles that make up an equilateral triangle, of which six form a hexagon. According to the Old Testament, King Solomon received 666 talents of gold per year from the temple. In kabbalistic and alchemical thinking, gold is associated with the Sun.

The three ancient names for the Sun are combined to form the name Solomon. The words "sol" in Latin, "om" in Hindi, and "on" in Egyptian all refer to the Sun. Additionally, the term contains three symmetrical placements of the vowel O. In addition to having a similar appearance to the Sun, O is the fifteenth letter in the English alphabet. From this we get, $\underline{O = 15 * 1 + 5 = 6}$, $\underline{O = 15 * 1 + 5 = 6}$, $\underline{O = 15 * 1 + 5 = 6}$ equals 666, the number of the Sun.

4	9	2
3	5	7
8	1	6

This square is unique such that each side totals 15 including the diagonals. (4 + 9 + 2 =15 [top row] and (4+5+6 = 15) [diagonal] and that the sum of the sides all equal 45.

This square was associated with the planet /god Saturn.

The rest of the planets had a square associated them moving in the Chaldean order: Jupiter 4x4, Mars 5x5, Sun 6x6, Venus 7x7, Mercury 8x8 and Moon 9x9.

6	32	3	34	35	1
7	11	27	28	8	30
19	14	16	15	23	24
18	20	22	21	17	13
25	29	10	9	26	12
36	5	33	4	2	31

If one totals each row or column of the square of the Sun/Sol, you will get (6+ 32 + 3 + 34 + 35 +1 =) 111.

35 + 8 +23 +17 + 26 + 2 = 111

If you sum the total of each of the sides you will get.....666!

Does it happen by chance that Jesus, the purported descendant of Solomon, also bears a symbol of the Sun?

Chapter 3: Concealed Concepts of the Bible

Lucifer's Connection to Venus and the Sun

The word Lucifer has often been misunderstood due to the Christian association with the Devil. The only Lucifer mentioned in the Bible, (and in very few Bible versions at that), is the King of Babylon addressed in Isaiah 14. In 382 A.D., the Hebrew word 'Hallel" was translated to Lucifer by St. Jerome.

The ancient Semites viewed the planet to be male in the morning and female in the evening, despite their knowledge that the morning and evening stars were distinct forms of the same entity. As a result, the morning star was referred to by the Romans as Lucifer, the bearer of light, who transformed into the evening sky's feminine Venus. In ancient times, the early light of dawn was personified as a goddess, the embodiment of Ishtar, Venus in the morning, who gloriously gave birth to the morning star, a magnificent male child who later changed into the rising Sun. As all the Sun gods initially represented, Lucifer was regarded as the god of light, a Sun god in Roman paganism that was only a metaphor of the light within each of us. The Sun is then depicted as gleaming in his power as the rays emerge.

HALLELUJAH = Praise of The Sun

There is a very ancient connection between self-praise and the Sun's lights' bursting intensity, roaring in splendour and victory. The Hebrew word "sahal" means "to cry out loud" as well as "to shine brightly." The names 'Halel," the Hebrew for morning star, and 'Hillel," the Arabic for 'New Moon," both indicate that the word 'Hillel," which also means to "cry out in triumph," originally meant "to be brilliant." As a verb, "el" in Hebrew means to shine, glitter, or irradiate; as a noun, it means splendour, irradiation, glory, and so on. That it is the origin of the Hebrew name for the Book of Psalms, which is filled with numerous references to worshipping the Sun. It is found in the term "hallelujah" and in all of the texts on Sun worship.

- JE-HALEL-EEL, a shout of adoration for the Sun or Sun God, was an ancient term for Sun worship. Jehiel, God's appraiser. In fact, his name meant the Sun in many Khitan households, and this Helios is Halel or Lucifer. However, the Khitan often used the same term to refer to the Moon and the Sun. Therefore, Jehaliel or Halel is just Lucifer, the one who brings light, day or night. Hittite is the source of the Latin word Sun and the Greek term helios.
- Hebrew Helel means "bright," Finnic Hel means "bright," and the Greek Helios means "Sun." HEL is an old root meaning "to shine." Sal, sometimes known as Sil, is the same in several languages, and the soft H is interchangeable with S: Akkadian and Turkish words for "Sun" are "sil" and "shine."

Two times "Hallelu-Yah" (הַלְלוּ יָהּ), cropped from the manuscript - French 13th Century

Lucifer and Jesus

In addition to being the Sun's hieroglyph, O was also its original name. Think about biblical titles like O God, O Lord, O Jesus, O Day Star, and O Lucifer if you know this. "How you are fallen from heaven, O Day star, son of dawn." - Isaiah 14:12-15. Herds of fanatics started referring to the devil by Isaiah 14 in the years that followed, and the name Lucifer somehow came to be associated with Satan. However, most modern interpreters carefully avoid the relationship since demonology is as messed up as the devil himself.

The devil has never been called Lucifer. On the contrary, in Revelation 22:16, the Christian saviour Jesus Christ is described as saying, "I am the bright morning star," meaning Lucifer. There was also a Christian sect in the fourth century CE known as the Luciferians, and one of the first popes of Rome had that name. Books such as the Book of Enoch, which employed a number of titles to depict the Devil, are the reason why the terms were used interchangeably until later Christianity. The Beast, Lucifer, Satan, and Beelzebub, for example

- The word "Lucifer" means "Light bringer" or "Light Bearer" and is also a title reserved for Jesus. For centuries, the Church used this word to refer to Jesus.
- Revelation 22:16, KJV - **"I am the root and the offspring of David, and the bright and morning star."**
- Isaiah 14:12, English Standard Version - **"How you are fallen from heaven, O'Day-Star, son of Dawn!"**
- **Day-star \da-star (1): Morning Star (2): The Sun**

According to the Freemasons, it is the all-seeing eye of Lucifer, Ra, Horus, or Osiris. This eye is unquestionably the symbol of the Sun or Sun God, as we know from the solar myths. The Sun was referred to as Mithra's eye in Vedic India. The two regions were then illuminated by Horus's two eyes. Because the two eyes were the Moon at night and the Sun at day. The Sun and Moon were sometimes referred to as the "eyes of Horus." (*Jesus = Rising Sun, Lucifer = Sun of the Dawn, Horus = Rising Sun, Mithra = Sun of Dawn*)

Speaking of Jesus, Revelation 1:14 states that "his eyes were like a flame of fire," which is also the case in Daniel 10:5–6. "His eyes are like flaming torches." The most ancient and widely used solar symbol appears to have been the eye, even though the Canaanite symbol for the Sun was an upright stone. The ancient belief that the Sun was all-seeing and that all that was visible to man was revealed by its penetrating glance naturally suggested and agreed to this symbol. All of the qualities of a phenomenal eye were, in essence, present in the Sun to ancient minds.

The eye has long been used to symbolise the Sun. For instance, the eye of Ra represented the Sun.

Chapter 4: The Book of Revelation and Astrotheology (1)

The Book of Revelation - Astrotheology (1)

- "To the angel of the church in Sardis write: These are the words of him who holds the seven spirits of God and the seven stars. I know your deeds; you have a reputation of being alive, but you are dead." - **Revelation 3:1**

- The Seven Stars: Often referred to as the Big Dipper, Ursa Major is a constellation composed of seven stars. The Bear and the Plough is another name for this constellation. It is still referred to as the Chariot of Souls or Spirits in France.
- It is being proposed that the seven Elohim in Hebrew Genesis are the same individuals and types as the seven Rishis of India, and that their astounding origins can be traced back to the seven major stars of the bear. Among these are the seven spirits of the Great Bear, which can be found in Egypt, China, and Japan; the seven Khnum, or pygmy sons of Ptah; the seven Kabiri; the seven Achaemenid clans; the seven princes of hell; the seven titans with Cronus; the seven Greek Heliades, or sons of Helios; the seven Hathors; the seven cows; Ra, with his seven souls; the seven pillars of wisdom; the seven gates in the cave of Mithras; the seven steps of the Masonic ladder; the candlestick with seven branches; the seven enclosures of the Jewish temple; the seven tablets and the seven spirits before the throne. The constellation Cassiopeia is the throne. This constellation is just in front of Ursa Major.

- "John to the seven churches which are in Asia: Grace be unto you, and peace, from him which is, and which was, and which is to come; and from the seven Spirits which are before his throne;" - **Revelation 1:4-7**
- "From the throne came flashes of lightning, rumblings and peals of thunder. In front of the throne, seven lamps were blazing. These are the seven spirits of God. Also in front of the throne there was what looked like a sea of glass, clear as crystal." - **Revelation 4-5**

- Therefore, in front of the throne where God sits in glory, there are seven burning symbol lamps. According to the author, the sky is a sea of glass that resembles a crystal. In the Middle Ages, the throne and Cassiopeia constellations were shown as Christ seated on his throne.

Church of the Monastery of St Anthony the Great. Coptic. 12th Century

- "(1) After this I looked, and there before me was a door standing open in heaven. And the voice I had first heard speaking to me like a trumpet said, "Come up here, and I will show you what must take place after this." (2) At once I was in the Spirit, and there before me was a throne in heaven with someone sitting on it. (3) And the one who sat there had the appearance of jasper and ruby. A rainbow that shone like an emerald encircled the throne." - **Revelation 4:1-3**

Nearly every mediaeval star chart features the person seated on the throne. These maps all show Cassiopeia in a regal position. Many 16th-century star charts feature the enthroned figure, typically in the Milky Way's centre. The throne is surrounded by a rainbow, according to the Apocalypse.

- "And there was a rainbow round about the throne in sight like unto an emerald." - **Revelation 4:3**

- The rainbow is a fairly accurate representation of the bright Milky Way, which forms an arch over the night sky. The clear resemblance of the enthroned person's description with a gemstone—we are informed that it resembled sardine and jasper—confirms the idea that the images are taken from the skies. It is quite natural and acceptable to compare the Sun and stars to glowing gemstones.
- Additionally, note that Sardian, which comes from the Greek word "sardinian," which means "red," is a blood-red gem. Revelation 21:11 states that jasper, a dense, opaque, cryptocrystalline form of quartz, is "clear as crystal."
- And since we know that it is Christ who sits on the throne, and that Jesus Christ is simply a metaphor for the Sun. It can hence be stated with confidence that the Jasper and sardine mentioned are representative descriptions of the Sun. Jasper appears as the color white and is symbolic of the bright white light of day. Sardine is typical of the red flame colored setting Sun. Imagine a gigantic Jasper and Sardine stone of human or greater dimensions, and think what its appearance would be. It would be white light mingled

with red fire. What is that but the Sun? Also worthy of examination is the fact that Sardine and Jasper were the first and last stones on the breastplate of the high priest Aaron.

- "And thou shalt set in it settings of stones, even four rows of stones. The first row shall be a sardius, a topaz, and a carbuncle. This shall be the first row and the second row shall be an emerald, a sapphire, and a diamond, and the third row a ligure, an agate, and an amethyst and the fourth row a beryl and an onyx and a Jasper." - **Exodus 28:17**

- Philo and Josephus recognised that the 12 zodiacal signs corresponded to the 12 tribes of Israel and the 12 stones of the breastplate. According to Philo, the 12 jewels on the priestly breastplate stand in for the signs of the solar zodiac, which are arranged to match the four seasons of the solar year. Philo makes no reference to months in this periscope. The Sun, or the tropical year, which is separated into seasons, solstices, and equinoxes, is the subject of this cosmological reference. The breast's 12 stones, which are arranged in four rows of threes and vary in colour. What else are they supposed to represent? However, when the zodiac circle is broken down into four parts, the seasons—spring, summer, autumn, and winter—are represented by three signs in each section. The Sun's revolutions inform us of the transition in each of those four, which is dictated by three signs. Medieval maps occasionally directly showed the connection between the constellation of Cassiopeia and Christ, to which the Apocalypse truly alludes. For instance, an image of a throne with the crucified Cassiopeia on it may be seen in the

Book of Ratdolt. The figure's hands are pinned to the throne, which has a cross-like back. It's clear that this is a Christian crucifix. Therefore, the Apocalypse contains references to the constellation of Cassiopeia, which was actually perceived as the stellar image of Christ the King enthroned in the Middle Ages.

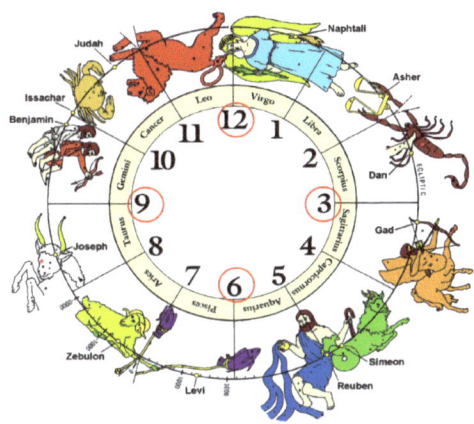

"Around about the throne were four and 20 seats, and upon the seats I saw four and 20 elders sitting clothed in white raiment, and they had on their heads crowns of gold." - **Revelation 4:4**

- The sky was formerly divided into 24 wing-shaped segments, or 24 meridional sectors that merged at the celestial sphere's poles, as any comprehensive astronomy textbook would point out. Direct stellar ascension hours or sidereal hours are other names for these sectors. The celestial coordinate system is defined by the 24 hours. Therefore, according to the equatorial system of coordinates—which is the dividing norm for the celestial sphere in astronomy—each elder of the Apocalypse seems to be a star hour. The elders white attire is only a reflection of the sky's white stars.
- The constellation of the northern crown, Corona Borealis, which is located in the zenith, or precisely over the heads of all 24 elders or sections, is presumably what the golden crowns are referring to.

- "Also in front of the throne there was what looked like a sea of glass, clear as crystal. In the center, around the throne, were four living creatures, and they were covered with eyes, in front and in back." - **Revelation 4:6**

- This describes the celestial sphere, which is filled with stars or eyeballs, that encircles the constellation of the Throne. The once cryptic reference to the place surrounding the throne becomes evident. In addition to the tiny stars strewn around the background, the throne's actual constellation is being addressed. What does it mean, however, that they were for living things and had eyes? A brief glance at a star chart makes this obvious.

The Mausoleum of Galla Placidia - Built Between 425 and 450

- "And the first beast was like a lion, and the second beast like a calf, and the third beast had a face as a man, and the fourth beast was like a flying eagle." - **Revelation 4:7**

- The first beast symbolises the summer solstice and is found in the constellation of Leo. Taurus the Bull, the second beast, was the one that brought about the vernal equinox, or spring, in that age. At the winter solstice, Aquarius, the Waterman, emerged as the third beast. The observer will see that the eagle has been used in place of the scorpion in the Bible. The Phoenix, a sign of transformation and spiritual rebirth, the Scorpion, and the Eagle are the only three signs found in the Scorpio constellation.
- The various Israelite tribes held the zodiac signs on their standards, with the exception of the scorpion, which Dan substituted for the eagle. The four signs of Joseph, Judah,

Reuben, and Dan were positioned at the four corners, and they are Taurus, Leo, Aquarius, and Scorpio, or the eagle. When the equinox fell in Taurus, the bull, the four cards were ordinal points of the sphere during the equinoxes and solstices.

- However, the fall equinox was represented by the eagle Aquila. At cardinal points of a particular zodiac sign, each season jumps ahead. Due to the equinox's precession, the cardinal points used to be in Taurus for spring, Leo for summer, Eagle for fall, and Aquarius for victory. Additionally, the two solstices—summer and winter—and the two equinoxes—spring and autumn—are the cardinal points. Four to five thousand years ago, the constellations that were located at the four cardinal points of the zodiac were these symbolic animals. The cross sign originated from these cardinal points.

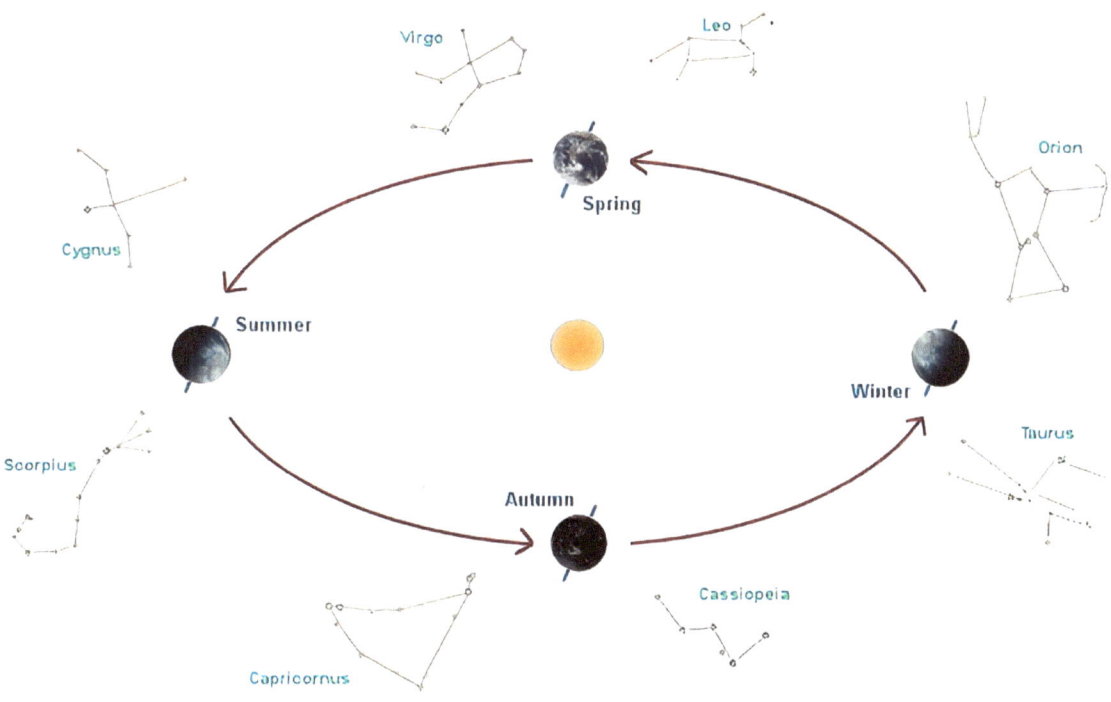

4 Seasonal Cardinal Points of the Zodiac

Chapter 5: The Book of Revelation and Astrotheology (2)

The Book of Revelation - Astrotheology (2)

Moreover, an occurrence of suspicion is revealed by the author of the Apocalypse, as we find in the Old Testament, in the Book of Ezekiel, the very same description of the same atmosphere and the same four creatures of the Zodiac.

- "And I looked, and, behold, a whirlwind came out of the north, a great cloud, and a fire infolding itself, and brightness was about it, and out of the midst thereof as the color of amber, out of the midst of the fire. Also out of the midst thereof came the likeness of four living creatures.... As for the likeness of their faces, they four had the face of a man, and the face of a lion, on the right side: and they four had the face of an ox on the left side; they four also had the face of an eagle." - **Ezekiel 1:4-10**
- Although it is abundantly clear that the author of the Apocalypse often used the books of Ezekiel and the Zodiac, it is more doubtful that both writers were exiled—Ezekiel to Babylon and John to the island of Patmos. Thus, the four major zodiac constellations—Leo, Taurus, Aquarius, and the Eagle—are explicitly listed in the Apocalypse. The seasons are represented by a cross or square of constellations. However, each of these animal constellations has precisely six sectors of direct ascension since there are exactly 24 star sectors, or wings, that extend from the pole. In other words, they are surrounded by six wings. Stated differently, each animal constellation is situated inside the area of the celestial sphere that is encompassed by these six sector wings.

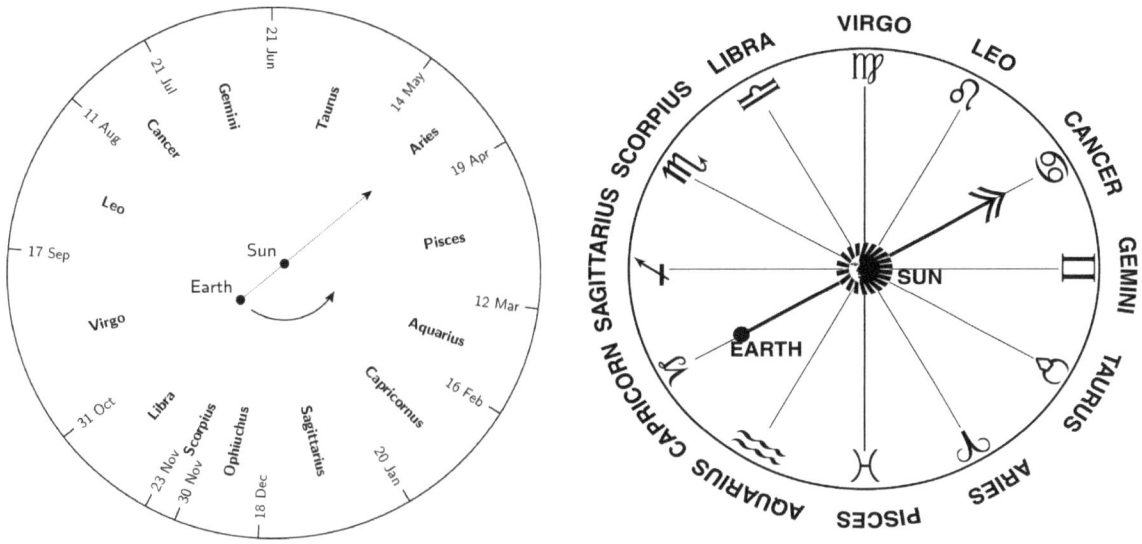

- "And the four beasts had each of them six wings about him, and they were full of eyes within the eyes." - **Revelation 4:8**

- The stars are shown here. This is, incidentally, phrased as within and around in the Greek text. These animals, which have eyeballs all over them, are most likely constellations. Consequently, the eyes in question ought to be stars. In fact, any mediaeval star chart depicts them in exactly this manner.

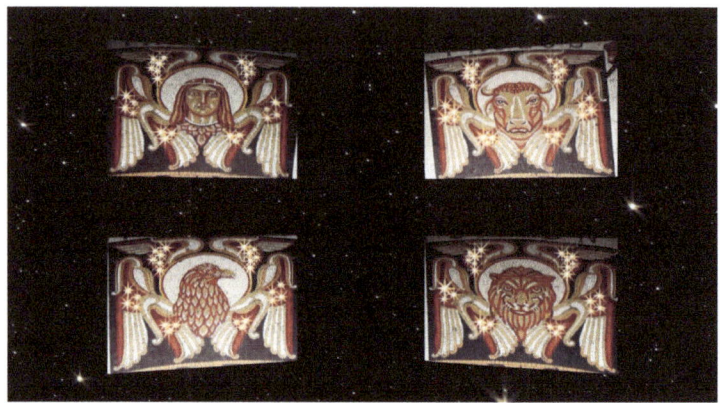

- "And I saw in the right hand of him that sat on the throne, a book written within, and on the backside sealed with seven seals." - **Revelation 5**
- "Behold, the Lion of the tribe of Juda, the Root of David, hath prevailed to open the book, and to loose the seven seals thereof. And I beheld, and, lo, in the midst of the throne and of the four beasts, and in the midst of the elders, stood a Lamb as it had been slain, having seven horns and seven eyes, which are the seven Spirits of God sent forth into all the Earth." - **Revelation 5**

- Leo is represented by the lion, and Aries by the lamb. One thing to note in this case is that the lion and the lamb are the same. The Apocalypse says that the former could open the book of the seven seals, but as the imitation celebrates the vernal Sun, or Aries, rather than the summer solstice, Sun, or lion, that role falls on the Lamb. In actuality, the Sun's complete power is embodied by these two symbolic animals. Beautiful and dazzling under Aries. Warm, passionate, and energising under Leo.
- In the majority of ancient cultures, the Sun appears as distributing light to Earth by travelling daily from east to west in a golden chariot pulled by the best and fastest horses.

"Praise to the Sun that rides four horses on his rapid course", according to the ancient Persians' sacred texts. As a result, horses were sacrificed to the Sun and considered sacred by the Persians. Curtius recounts a similar parade in which white horses pulled the chariot dedicated to Jupiter. It was followed by a horse of extraordinary size, which they called the horse of the Sun. Herodotus says; "they sacrifice horses to the Sun," which is the only object of their religion. This tradition is based on the belief that the fastest animal should be given to the fastest god. According to Isidore of Seville, the Romans presented the Sun with a chariot pulled by four horses, each of which was supposed to symbolise the four elements and the four seasons by its colour.

- The Sun has four. It is a rule which cannot be deviated from a rule established by antiquity for very good reasons. The four horses are symbols of the four different appearances of the Sun and of the four seasons. Their names prove it. According to Fulgentius, they are called Erythrinus the Red, the Luminous Lampos the Resplendent, and Pythagoras the friend of the Earth, which relate manifestly to the different degrees and appearances of the solar light.

- [1] "And I saw when the Lamb opened one of the seals, and I heard, as it were the noise of thunder, one of the four beasts saying, Come and see. [2] And I saw, and behold a white horse: and he that sat on him had a bow; and a crown was given unto him: and he went forth conquering, and to conquer." - **Revelation 6:2**
- The four horses are, first and foremost, the Sun's messengers. They are coloured according to the season, and the rider, who rides a white horse, is always seen as the good guy. He wields a bow and wears a crown. As a conqueror determined to conquer, he rides off. The planet is rejuvenated in the spring. With its warmth and vitality, our hero, the

Sun, defeated the winter's darkness, cold, and death. Observe how he is facing the other direction in the spring, aiming his bow towards winter.

- The word crown, which comes from the Latin root word corona, was originally used to symbolise the Sun's golden rays and to connect the ruler with the Sun's power and right to govern. The Sun is exalted in this house and in Aries, thus the rider wears the crown. He is known as the Sun that conquers. To save us, Jesus resurrected from the dead—the dead of winter. His bow is a long-standing representation of numerous Sun gods. The bow and arrow is displayed by Mithras, Helios, Hercules, Saturn, Marduk, Krishna, and most importantly Apollo. The Sun's energy, rays, and fertilising and purifying properties are symbolised by Apollo's bow and arrow. Here, the bow symbolises his, the Sun's, and spring's plans to defeat winter and death. The Sun will rise again.

- "When the Lamb opened the second seal, I heard the second living creature say, "Come!" Then another horse came out, a red one. Its rider was given power to take away peace from the Earth and to make people kill each other, and he was given a big sword." - **Revelation 6:3-4**

- The summer Sun and season are represented by the red horse and its rider. The Greek word pyros, which means fire, is the source of the word red in this instance, confirming the sign of the summer's intense heat. Furthermore, he was granted the authority to destroy the peace on Earth and to murder each other, but this authority does not extend to any hatred amongst people. It makes reference to the Sun's destructive nature. The Sun may sometimes be just as harmful as it is helpful. It was given to him a big sword, and its rays may easily sear the ground, produce drought, and leave crops withered and dead. Additionally, locust swarms typically occur after severe drought or towards the end of summer. Once more, the Sun is represented by the sword. The sword is often only used as a symbol of martial values, especially manly, sweet courage and strength. As a result, it also represents power and the Sun in relation to the dynamic masculine essence and the Sun's piercing, darting rays that resemble swords. The summer heat transformed into a lion that devoured our ancestors.

Folio 7v of an Apocalypse Manuscript - The Red Horse of the Apocalypse and Its Rider

- "When he ripped off the third seal, I heard the third Animal cry, "Come out!" I looked. A black horse this time. Its rider carried a set of scales in his hand. I heard a message (it seemed to issue from the Four Animals): "A quart of wheat for a day's wages, or three quarts of barley, but don't lay even a finger on the oil and wine." - **Revelation 6:5-6**

- This verse provides us with a wonderful glimpse of the astronomical state, which we will later recognise and value. When the Sun has crossed the equinox and the days are getting shorter and darker, the black horse symbolises the autumn or autumnal season, which is when we can clearly see the dark approach of winter. The Sun descends below the equator as the constellation Libra approaches its death at the winter solstice, and the scales sit in for the constellation.

- The fall equinox, when day and night are equal in length, is symbolised by scales. The equator has six months above it and six months below it. The six months above which are positive and life-affirming are represented by one band of the scale. The white horse and the other band therefore stand for the six months below, which are depressing and life-effacing. The black horse, this horseman is told, "a measure of wheat for a penny and three measures of barley for a penny, exhorting over the abundance after harvest and the cheapness of bread, the staff of life". All this means is that bread is the staple of life worldwide, so keep your stockpile in reserve. Winter will arrive soon. The ancient people may likely freeze to death over the next winter months if they had not saved enough food by this time of year. They were also warned to use care since some of the items, namely grapes and olives, were not yet ripe or mature enough for wine and oil. "Fancy thou hurt not the oil and the wine," they said.

Four Horsemen of the Apocalypse, an 1887 painting by Viktor Vasnetsov

- "And when he had opened the fourth seal, I heard the voice of the fourth beast say, Come and see. And I looked, and behold a pale horse: and his name that sat on him was Death, and Hell followed with him. And power was given unto them over the fourth part of the Earth, to kill with sword, and with hunger, and with death, and with the beasts of the Earth." - **Revelation 6:7-8**

- The pale horse refers to the winter season, when death seems to strike all vegetable life, while the forth rider's death is a reflection of the headed Sun. The once green and flourishing grass has turned brown and wilting. No flower dares to open its petals to the storm, and no bud dares to blossom in any field. Among the trees without leaves, the chilly winds continue to groan. The sound of the birds and all bug life is stifled. Like adamant rocks, the Earth is frozen. Hence the proverb "dead of winter." The Greek word Hades is the source of the English word "hell" in the Bible. The fairly recent idea of a Christian flaming hell has been incorrectly associated with the word Hades. In reality, the

Greek name Hades refers to the cold, dark underworld—a dreary, dark netherworld that is separated from God.

- The scorpion and Sagittarius are signs for the river of Hades, which is the part of the Milky Way's starry stream that lies below the equator and through which the Sun travels in October and November. The ancient priests of the Sun, the realm of the dead, and the winter months called this part of the zodiac Hades.

The Hades Amphora, depicting Hades (right) and Persephone (left). Painted by "The Oionokles Painter - 470 BC

According to legend, he was followed by either Hades or hell. As to the Apocalypse, "power was given onto them," referring to the pale horse and its rider over the fourth area of the Earth, which is the final quarter of winter on the Zodiac. The fourth horseman of death kills with each of the evil features of the previous horsemen. He uses the sword that was handed to the second Horseman of Summer to slay, and his choices have an effect that lasts throughout the winter. Since most natural life dies and starves in the winter, he destroys with hunger. And together with the Earth's beasts, he destroys. Some have referred to the constellations as the Earth's beasts. The Latin zodiacus or Greek zodiakos, which means little animals, is whence the words "zoo" and "zodiac" originate. In other words, man is killed not only by the terrible summertime hardships and Libra, whose scales lie below the equator into darkness, but also by all the beasts and the destructive traits of every sign of the zodiac. At the opening of the first four seals, the four living creatures repeatedly scream and come to observe. Make it known. The phrase "come and see" is mistranslated since it is only read as "come" in the Latin Vulgate and Greek Septuagint. The living creatures are not telling the author to come and see. The four horsemen are called to begin their assigned cardinal seasons by the four living beings that are fixed in spring, summer, autumn and winter.

Chapter 6: Unveiling the Alpha and Omega

The Alpha and Omega - Unveiled

Christ Jesus declared, "I am the Alpha and the Omega," says the Lord God, "who is, and who was, and who is to come, the Almighty."

According to Hindu literature, Ka is also the beginning and the end, the first and the last. According to the Gita, Krishna reportedly remarked, "I myself never was not." "Learn that he by whom all things were formed, meaning himself is incorruptible." "I am eternity and non eternity." "I am before all things and the mighty ruler of the universe." "I am the beginning, the middle and the end of all things." Consider that Krishna was worshipped for more than 3,000 years before the time of Jesus. We also learn that Vishnu, who took the shape of Krishna and entered Devaki's womb to become her son, had no beginning, middle, or end in the Vishnu Purana, another sacred text for Hindus.

Buddha has no beginning or end, and he is also Alpha and Omega. The almighty, all-powerful Lord is worthy of eternal thought. Eternal One, the Supreme Being. It should be mentioned that Buddha was worshipped for over 1,000 years before Christ.

The firstborn of the Eternal One, according to Zendavista or Muzd, is the one who is, has been, and will be forever. The Alpha and Omega were also Zeus. Zeus is at the beginning of an Orphic line, and Zeus is at the centre. Zeus is the creator of everything. Bacchus was without beginning or end. On an ancient medal dedicated to him, it is said, "It is I who leads you. It is I who protects you and who saves you. I am Alpha and Omega." This inscription or the Temple of Isis in Egypt are mentioned by Plutarch. "I am all that was and is and shall be, and my veil no mortal can remove."

The Alpha and Omega symbolised Taurus and the nearby Aries. The first spring equinoxes are Taurus, which is named Alap in Hebrew, and Aries, which is subsequently called Ayin (Oin). The first sign was especially connected to the last, the bull to the ram, as the letter replaced the former due to the equinoctial points' precession. Taurus and then Aries represented the God whose symbol was thought to be the spring equinox. However, in both cases, the Sun served as a real image of the deity.

Iao (Jehovah) rode on the cherub, also known as the Assyrian bull, which we understand to be travelling with the Sun in Taurus. Anu, Krishna, Hadad, and Lord Shiva are among the other gods that ride bulls. In proto-Canite, a bull is also called "Alp"; in Ugaritic, "Alpu"; in Phoenician, "Alp"; in Hebrew, "Alef"; in Greek "Alpha," "A," or "Aleph." In the Phoenician and Hebrew alphabets, the first letter was initially shaped to roughly represent a bull's horned head. It looked a lot like the English A upside down. It has long been used to convey a sense of power or energy. The bull and all of his strength were symbolised by the letter as the bull was meant to start the year with his horns at the vernal equinox. The Alpha and Omega, the Sun of unity and number, are represented by the letter "I," which I say to be the name of the Supreme Being. And "A" was and will be the Almighty Bull, Baal, the "first and the last, the beginning and the end."

Say it in every language spoken by any group on the planet, and disguise it as you choose. Its core and importance are derived from the name of the sacred animal in our own language, which is still Baal, the name of the highest God, when the covenant, or spring equinox, was in the bull of their zodiac. Thus demonstrating that the Sun is, and has been, the exclusive and supreme focus of all worship and the study of the Sun or astronomy. Freemasonry's inner and occult secret is the science of the Sun, which is the hidden meaning behind all enigmatic allegories and the Sun itself. Since Taurus was the first of the signs and the year began at the spring equinox, the sabaist's based their idolatrous worship on this chronological order. However, scientists must have realised that the solstices and equinoxes had moved into other signs due to the fixed stars' retrograde motion, and as a result, the adoration of the people for some symbols became out of place. At the spring equinox, the Sun therefore moved from the sign of Taurus to Aries, which in turn became the first constellation in the zodiac.

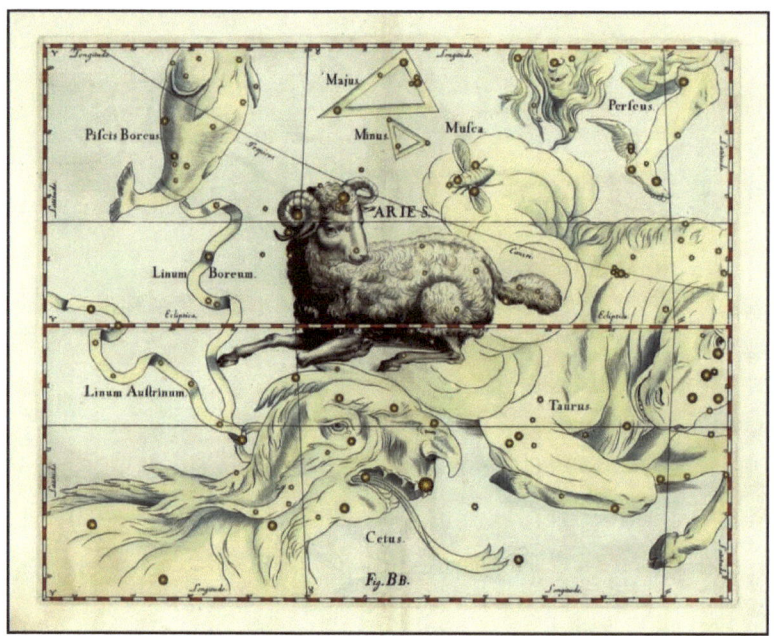

Throughout the Old Testament, the word "ayin" appears several times, most of which refer to the eye or eyesight. However, ayin can also refer to a spring, fountain, or water well. As the spring showers do at the vernal equinox or spring. The Old English word "springing" implies to leap, burst forth, fly up, spread, and flourish. Without a doubt, this watery notion of ayin is where our English term "spring" originates. Since their language lacked a comparable sound, the Greeks, who adopted the Phoenician alphabet, employed the Phoenician "A" as a sign for the necessary vowel "O." Both the omicron and omega sounds are represented by the letter "O" in the oldest Greek inscriptions. The closed form "O," often known as omicron or little "o," was briefly taken when the symbol underwent differentiation about 550 BC. To symbolise the long "O", often known as "Omega" or the "long O," it was expanded out at the bottom. All things considered, "Ayin" is a 360-degree circle eye. The letter "O" symbolises going back to the beginning, the beginning and the end, the first and the last. Thus, the relationship between Aries and Omega. Additionally, it should be noted that the astrological sign of Aries strongly resembles the lowercase letter of Omega when reversed. However, in the nations that believed that the Sun's yearly orbit around the sky began on the spring equinox, or when the Sun was in the zodiac's Lamb, the Lamb was regarded as the world's creator. And as you can see, the ecliptic crosses the equator exactly where the Lamb or ram of God is situated in the zodiac. As a result, the Lamb and the cross are now essentially and independently related concepts.

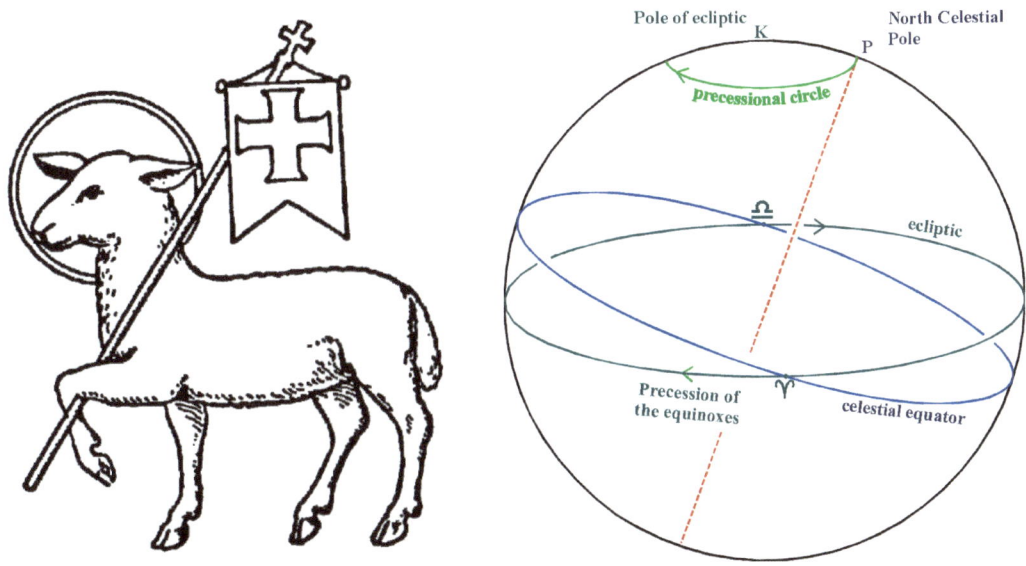

The Lamb was said to be crucified. So you get to the point of that verse in St. John where Jesus Christ, the Son, is described as having been crucified from the beginning of time; that is, he is crucified or crosses the equator every spring in the exact moment when the yearly cycle begins. The ancient practice of celebrating the crucifixion, or passover, when the Sun crossed the equator at the spring equinox and entered the lamb's zodiac sign of Aries, is where the association of the Sun, cross, and lamb first emerged.

The Babylonians, Egyptians, and Jews all used lambs in their sacrificial rites. In Bacchus's rites, a lamb was killed, with the animal standing in front of a cross with Sun rays or a solar disc surrounding its head. According to early Christian doctrine, the world's sins were atoned for by the blood of God's Lamb. The Church actively worked to establish its power and concepts, but it did not want to make the crucifixion a contentious issue. Furthermore, Jesus Christ was never seen hanging on a crucifixion for nearly seven centuries. Jesus on the crucifixion is not seen in any of the paintings found in the Roman tombs. Additionally, a lamb is used at Holy Sepulchre to symbolise the Saviour. This doctrine was eventually changed at the Trullo Council in Constantinople in 692 AD, and all crucifixes from that point on included the image of Jesus, but the Lamb was still visible, often at the base of the cross. Jesus was initially shown standing peacefully in front of the crucifixion with his arms outstretched, completely clothed. As Jesus is depicted on crucifixes today, he was later hung on the cross and ultimately shown undraped, bleeding, and tormented by the agony of his wounds.

Blood of Jesus Christ & The Mystic Lamb

The Sun's passage over or crossing of the equator in March, when the ram or Lamb of God was the zodiacal symbol, was symbolised by the crucifixion on Mount Calvary. God, the Sun was in that sign on the equinox of spring. The Jewish traditions of the Passover and the Paschal lamb originated here as well, and they originated from their Egyptian masters. Setting aside the ridiculous metaphor, the evangelist John's description of God, "the hair of his head was like wool," is an amazing depiction of the god. In March, the Sun was in the sign of Ram, and the constellation of Aries was worshipped throughout his transit through that sign. And for that precise reason, Jesus is always seen holding or cradling the lamb because he is the Sun. In Aries, it's only the Sun. Can one be that blind as to miss the god's history in all of this? IAO, IHS, Iesous, the Alpha and Omega, the incarnate God, and the Lamb of God offered as a sacrifice to atone for the world's sins. As one might anticipate, this saviour first appeared and worshipped as a lamb, which represents the Sun in Aries.

Chapter 7: The God of 1000 Names

Saturn = The Hidden God

For those who were initiated, Saturn represented the secret God, just as mystery denotes a concealed system. The God who had been hidden was unveiled to everyone else. The name Saturn is pronounced Satur in Chaldee, however it only has four letters. By using the value of the letters in the Hebrew or Chaldee alphabets, you can find the number 666 by Gematria. "Let the one with knowledge count the beast's number, since it is a man's, and he has three hundred and sixty-six." - Revelation 13:18.

The Greek name for Jesus is known as Iesous, and when applied to Gematria, Iesous equals 888 (Iseous = 888). But according to foundation 9 numerology, Jesus' name is worth 666 (J = 90, E = 45, S = 171, U = 189, S = 171, Total = 666). It should therefore come as no surprise that Agrippa's magic Sun square also equals 666, as Jesus is a symbol of the Sun. It is important to note that the fact that the Sun, Saturn, and Jesus all have this apocalyptic number is not a coincidence. The likelihood of discovering all three names that are associated with the number 666 is quite high, regardless of the numerological approach used.

It is important to remember that 666 is a number that alludes directly to the Sun or the beast that rises in the east. From a Babylonian perspective, 666 is the number of the God of Babylon and his successor, the Pope. Additionally, the Pope stands in for the current Saturn at the centre of the ancient mystery. Rome was formerly known as Saturnia, or the city of Saturn. Long before the mythical establishment of Rome, the representative of the mysteries of Babylon, who was based on Capitol and Hill, most likely gave it this name. As the leader of the Church of Rome's mysteries, the Pope names his church the Latin Church and requires that the same services be held in Latin.

Lateinos, which means "number of the beast," and Saturn have precisely the same meaning. "Latin" comes from the Greek "Lateinos," which means Saturn. Both have a connection with the God of Mystery or the Hidden One. 666 is the result of applying the Greek alphabet's letter values (L = 30, A = 1, T = 300, E = 5, I = 10, N = 50, O = 70, S = 200, Total = 666). All three words—Latium, Latinus, and the Roman version of the Greek Lateinos and Lateo, which imply to lie and hide—come from the Chaldean, which means the same thing. The great Babylonian God had clearly been given the name Lat, or the Hidden One, in addition to Saturn. The name of the fish lattice, which was worshipped alongside the Egyptian Minerva at the Egyptian city of Latiplus, makes this evident. As we have seen, Bacchus was named Ichthys, or the fish, and the Assyrian goddess Atargatis is claimed to have been thrown into the Ashkelon Lake with her son Ichthys. The Pope is the leader of the mystery of iniquity, and if he is, the genuine representation of Saturn, then his number is just 666. Furthermore, as we have seen, Rome itself was once known as Saturnia, or the city of Saturn.

Saturnalia (1783) by Antoine-François Callet

Therefore, the Pope is entitled to both the beast's name and number. In the city of the seven hills, where the Roman Saturn once ruled, he is the only authentic representation of the original Saturn that still exists. From his home, the entire Italian continent was referred to as the Saturnian land for a long time. However, what relevance does this have to the name Lateinos, which is widely thought to be the beast's name? It demonstrates that the general consensus is clearly established. In terms of importance and belonging to the same God, Saturn and Lateinos are simply interchangeable. The viewer will never forget Virgil's lines showing that Lateinos, to whom the Romans or Latin race attributed their ancestry, were shown with a glory around his head to demonstrate that he was a child of the Sun. It follows that the original Lateinos were seen by the general public as having held the same place as Saturn, who was as worshipped as the Sun's offspring in the mysteries.

Neptune Roman God - Bardo Museum, Roman Mosaic

Moreover, the fact that the Romans knew that the term Lateinos meant the "Hidden One" is evident from the fact that their historians claimed that Latium's name was derived from Saturn's "lying hid there." Even according to Roman testimony, Lateinos is the same as the Hidden One, or Saturn, the God of mystery. Lateinos, which also has the same number, is a strange and unique name for the same beast, whereas Saturn, which is the name of the beast, also contains the mystic number. The head of the Babylonian mystery, Lateinos, or Saturn, is just as much the head of the beast as the Pope. Its heavenly apocalyptic appellation, mystery, has been inscribed on the very forehead of his apostate communion by the Pope himself. The Great Babylon.

Therefore, it is obvious that the Pope is that man of sin. The Pope stands in for the hidden God, the God of the Mysteries, who is Saturnia, or the city of Saturn. The Pope, who holds the title of the Mystery, mandates that services of the Mystery performed in the Church of the Mystery be done in the Mystery's language!

Furthermore, it is no secret that the foundation of Christianity and its teachings was laid by the Roman Catholic Church. It has also been demonstrated and proven that Satan masquerades as Jesus Christ, the Son of the Sun, the Sun, and has a glory surrounding his head; thus, the hidden God Saturn.

Saturn The God of 1000 Names

Pagans have worshipped stars and planets in ancient times in an effort to honour or devour energy to their gods. In politics, religion, and daily customs, this kind of paganistic legacy persists to this day. The ancients worshipped Saturn for hundreds to thousands of years, and it is now thought that the world's political elite also worship it. Known as "El worship" in the past, Saturnian concepts are now deeply embedded in all religions and are important in black magic and occultism.

The cataclysmic disasters that are now occurring in this world hail from Saturn. The concept is crucial to theology, religion, and international relations. Several texts refer to Saturn as the "Sun," instead of using its usual astronomical name in Babylonian nomenclature. The mysterious practice of worshipping Saturn was common between 612 and 750 BC. The cults of the Sun and Moon are the next oldest, after the worship of Saturn. Several sources suggest that it would never have vanished since it is so deeply embedded in human traditions, and that its rituals are still performed today. Saturn is also known as Seth in the Ancient Egyptian religion and El in the Semitic nations. Hence, these titles just refer to the same deity, Satan, who is the equivalent of those names. It was depicted as a satyr—a half-human, half-goat creature—in Hellenistic culture. Consequently, Satan, the lord of darkness, took on Pan's cult and image later.

Pan (Greek Deity)   Baphomet (Deity)

Significance of Saturn

The six-sided hexagram near Saturn's North Pole is particularly important since Saturn is the sixth planet in our solar system. The brilliant light above our plane is the place of luminary expression, where the hexagram represents the revelation of the esoteric principles. The number 6 on the cube, which stands both materialism and spell casting, is an illustration of the hexagram.

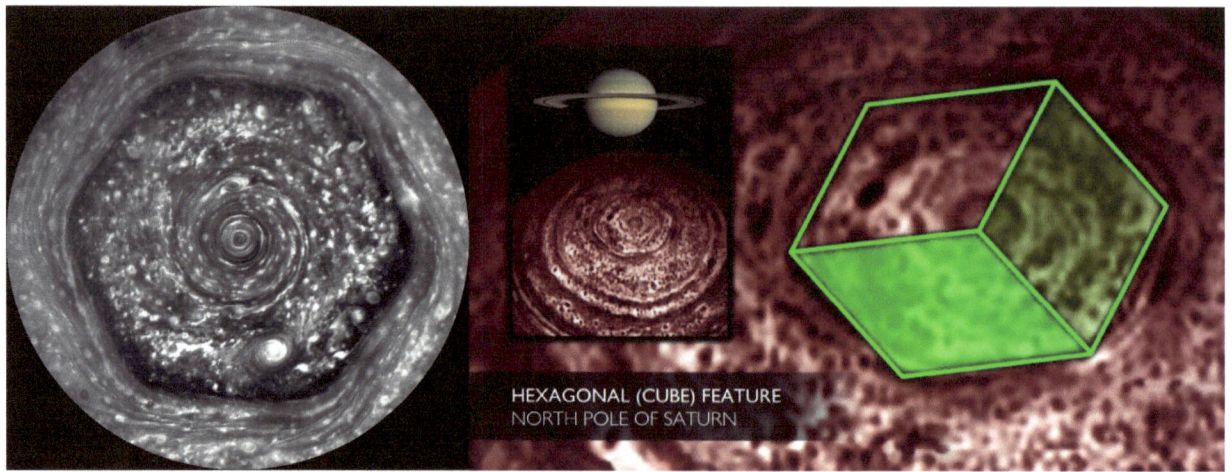

The hexagram was used in ceremonial and esoteric black magic rituals connected to Satanic and Saturnian worship, just as the pentagram. In the past, altars representing the pagan gods were made out of the esoteric geometric shape of the hexagram. The Ancient Rempha, also known as Chuin or Moloch, is symbolised by the hexagram or six-pointed star.

Acts 7:43 - "Yea, ye took up the tabernacle of Moloch, and the star of your god Remphan, figures which ye made to worship them: and I will carry you away beyond Babylon."

- **In Amos 5:26, the God of Israel mentioned and condemned the star, referring to it as "the star of your god, Moloch" or "Chiun." Acts 7:43 also made a reference to**

Amos 5:26 and the Israelites having it in the wilderness. It was known as the Star of Remphan. The "god" Saturn is referred to by all these names.

- **"But ye have borne the tabernacle of your Moloch and Chiun your images, (Gods of Saturn) the star of your god which ye made for yourselves." (KJ12)**

The use of Saturnian concepts is made abundantly clear throughout the Bible and various religious texts.

The effect of Saturn's geometric shape is exemplified by "The Planetary Ritual of the Hexagram". It starts by using solar forces and then moves through the conventional planetary sequence, following the Rituals of the Pentagram, using elemental energies. One of the traditional practices was to attribute the six-pointed star to Saturn and use its energy fields. Most people utilise the six-pointed star as a talisman and to call out demons and spirits from the lowest planes of the spiritual world.

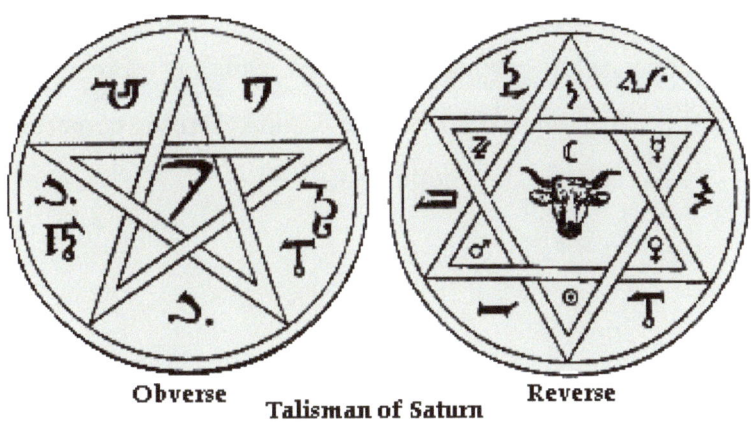

Obverse   Talisman of Saturn   Reverse

 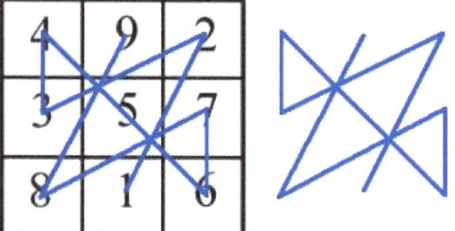

Figure 7- The Sigil of Saturn produces a unique symmetric pattern. The Sigil is shown here both overlaid upon the Freemasons' Magic Square, and by itself.

(1) The Freemasonic square and compass symbol, which is a symbol used in the prestigious craft of Freemasonry, appears in the center of the hexagram. Spell casting is also referred to as a "Hex."

(2) The square and compass are made up of the Sigil of Saturn that is displayed on the Magic Square, which again uses Saturnian symbolism.

- "The interlacing triangles or deltas symbolize the union of the two principles or forces, the active and passive, male and female, pervading the universe ... The two triangles, one white and the other black, interlacing, typify the mingling of apparent opposites in nature, darkness and light, error and truth, ignorance and wisdom, evil and good, throughout human life." – **Albert G. Mackey: Encyclopedia of Freemasonry**

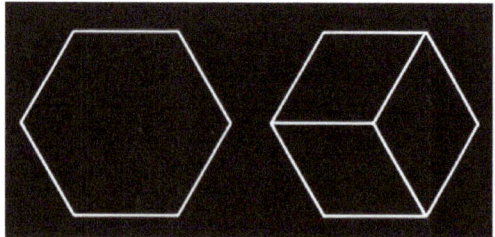 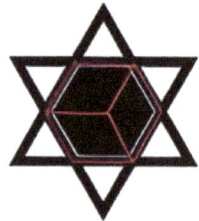 

Since the Phenocane, Satanists have worshiped Saturn, which is represented by a hexagram, cube, or star with six sides. To honor veterans, the Satanic Temple constructed a black cube monument.

Saturn As The Original or Second Sun

Why does every ancient culture name Saturn as the first and best Sun?

Saturn was linked to numerous gods, including Shamash, Atum, Helios, Cronus, Ra, An, Odin, Yahweh, Triptolemos, Quetzalcoatl, Moloch, the wheel of Buddha, Kolob, the first king, the dying or displaced god, the motionless "Sun," the unity of "heaven," the "great conjunction" of the golden age, the "cosmic wheel" stationary at the polar north, and many more. Once the polar configuration broke apart, the connected planets traveled and were trapped into the new orbit we observe today, leaving behind archetypes and morphological traits that gave rise to the planet.

Saturn used to be ringless. Earth also did at once. Saturn's rings are quite young, having formed maybe as recently as 100 million years ago. During the worldwide flood, Saturn dumped water on Earth, forming the ice and water rings that are seen today. There are further rings on Jupiter that are only visible with specific magnetic spectra. Even without the Sun, Saturn still produces heat, despite scientists' belief that it should have done so long ago.

Saturnalia was the old name for Christmas. The current Sun (Sunday, the "new sabbath") and Moon (Monday, when there was no Moon) were added later, and each day of the week is named after one of the five original planets. The sixth day of the week is Saturnsday, or Saturday, the first sabbath. The evolution of letters and number systems was influenced by the motion of planets accompanied by plasma discharge as observed in the ancient sky. The names of the months of the year are also based on planets and occurrences. In the past, our year included 365.2422 days. After 360 days, the crescent's polar structure underwent a full circumferential rotation. When the heliosphere of the present Sun appeared, it illuminated the planets, which were then referred to as stars.

Because it was a satellite of Saturn, Earth was formerly referred to as the "Night Sun" during the period when the Sun was closest to Saturn. Proto-Saturn, without its continuous rings, was far closer to the Sun. Since Saturn's orbit is elliptical, like that of all other planets, there are times when it is closer to the Sun than others. When Saturn is in its nova-like phase, it is commonly called a Night Sun. There is detailed mythology about Saturn, commonly referred to as the "Black Sun" or the "Second Sun," which was revered in antiquity and has many cultural allusions around the world.

According To Scholars, Saturn Was Formerly Revered As The Night Sun

(1977) Dwardu Cardona wrote:

"Diodorus Siculus was not the only writer of antiquity who stated that the Babylonians called Saturn the "Sun star."(19) Hyginus also expressed his opinion that Saturn was called "the star of the Sun. (20) Among modern Assyriologists, it seems as if Thompson was one of the first to notice that the Babylonians designated the planet Saturn as Shamash. (21) Yet Shamash, as a cursory glance through any work on Assyro-Babylorian mythology will show, was, very much like the Egyptian Ra, the usual Babylonian name for the Sun."(5] - **Dwardu Cardona, "The Sun Of Night," Kronos Vol. III No. 1 (Fall 1977)**

(1975) Lewis M. Greenberg and Warner B. Sizemore wrote:

".. the planet Saturn was designated as Shamash or "Sun" by the Assyro-Babylonian astrologers; and as far back as 1910 M. Jastrow (Revue d'Assyriologie, Vol. 70, p. 171)[3] proposed "the idea that Saturn was a 'steady' or 'permanent' mock-Sun – performing the same function of furnishing light at night that Sama's – the Sun performed during the day. .. Furthermore, there is undeniable evidence that the concept of a "night-Sun" as well as a "day-Sun" existed in Ancient Babylonian astrological thought."[4] - **Lewis M. Greenberg and Warner B. Sizemore, "Saturn And Genesis," Kronos Vol. I No. 3 (Fall 1975)**

(1979) Immanuel Velikovsky wrote:

"My conclusion that, as a result of its interplay with Jupiter, Saturn became a nova,(7) I found confirmed in many ancient sources, in which Saturn is regularly associated with brilliant light; but I was led to this idea first of all by a certain clue contained in the Biblical account of the Deluge." - **Immanuel Velikovsky, "On Saturn And The Flood," Kronos Vol. V No. 1 (Fall 1979)**

Earth As A Satellite of Saturn

Independently, a number of authors have proposed that mythological sources and ancient texts lead to the conclusion that the Earth was once a Saturnian Moon:

(1977) Harold Tresman and Bernard Newgrosh (writing as B. Geoghan) wrote:
"What must have been the relationship between the Earth and this great body – proto-Saturn? There are two answers we consider. The first is that the Earth was indeed nearer to this body, but on an orbit about the Sun independent of the great body, thus there would be times when the aspect of the proto-Saturn body would be large. However, there would also be times when its aspect would be quite small, as at present. Neither does this explanation account for some of the satellitic descriptions. The alternative proposal is startling. It is that at one time the Earth orbited as a satellite of proto-Saturn." [19] - **Tresman, Harold & B. O'Gheoghan (1977), "The Primordial Light," SIS. Review Vol II No 2 (December), 35-40.**

(1974) Lynn E. Rose writes:
"Still others may suppose that the pre-flood 'year' was indeed the period of Earth's revolution, but that Earth was revolving around somebody other than the Sun (7)." [18] - **Lynn E. Rose, "The Lengths of the Year", Pensée Vol. 4 No 3: (Summer 1974) "Immanuel Velikovsky Reconsidered VIII. Referencing: Frederic B. Jueneman, "A Most Exciting Planet," Industrial Research, 15 (July, 1973), p. 11.**

(1977) Ralph E. Juergens wrote:
"Velkovsky has stated that Saturn was disrupted in a near-collision with Jupiter. Knowing little or nothing of the details, I can most easily imagine such an encounter in terms of a Saturnian planetary system, which included the Earth, being invaded, dismembered, and captured by an interloping system of relative giants consisting essentially of the present Sun and Jupiter (if nothing else, the axial inclinations of Jupiter and its offspring, Venus, argue for an ancestral relationship between Jupiter and the Sun). Now, even though Velikovsky points out that Saturn was once a much more massive body than it is today, it is hard to imagine that it could have been massive enough to be a star in the context of the thermonuclear theory of stellar energy. If,

82

however, it was an electrically fuelled star, its initial stellar state and its sudden demise seem readily explainable." - **Ralph E. Juergens, "The Critics and Stellar Energy," SIS Review Vol II No 2 (Dec 1977)**

(1979) Immanuel Velikovsky wrote:

"It is conceivable that the Earth was, at that time, a satellite of Saturn, afterwards possibly becoming a satellite of Jupiter." [22] - **Ibid. Velikovsky 1979**

(1978) Dwardu Cardona wrote:

"It is also possible that the planet Saturn was much closer to Earth than it is at present or that the Earth itself was on an entirely different orbit and at a different distance from the Sun than it is now. In fact we have good reason to believe that, during the period of Earth history with which we are concerned, our little world was actually a satellite held in the electro-magnetic and/or gravitational embrace of the giant planet." [2] - **Dwardu Cardona, "Let There be Light," Kronos Vol. III No. 3 (Spring 1978)**

(1980) David Talbott wrote in his book, The Saturn Myth:

"Saturn did not move on its present remote orbit, but ruled as the central Sun around which the other heavenly bodies visually revolved."

These explanations might shed light on the reason why many ancient texts refer to Saturn as the Sun. The ancient symbols also have a significant impact on how the ancients perceived Saturn in the night sky.

Fig. g
Solar Symbol at Uxmal (Publications of the *Bureau of Ethnography*. vol. ii., pl. 57, No. 5) from Goblet, p. 226.

Fig. h
A composite of Saturn imagery (drawn by D. Talbott). In terms of Solaria Binaria, the view is up the Magnetic Tube from Earth.

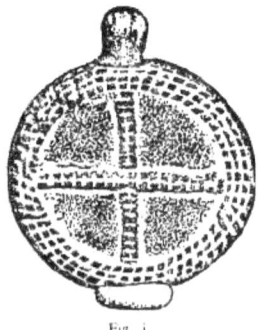

Fig. i
Pendant called "The Female Sun."

*From Fisher H. Mesmith, Jr., (1979) "Dogon Bronzes," XII *African Arts*, No. 2, (Feb.) 23.

The Worship of Saturn: The Unwitting Religion That Everyone Worships

You might be surprised to learn that Saturn has been worshipped for thousands of years globally. The rituals of the religion are still performed today, and it has never stopped. All of humanity regarded Saturn as the greatest god and king-ruler before the Great Flood.

"Chronos, or Saturn, Dionysos, Hyperion, Atlas, Hercules, were all connected with 'a great Saturnian continent;' they were kings that ruled over countries on the western shores of the Mediterranean, Africa and Spain." **– Baldwin, Prehistoric Nations**

The Roman god of time, Kronos (or can be spelt Cronus), is equated to the ruler of Saturn. The word "Satan" comes from the word "Saturn," which means "ruler of Father Time" in Latin. The Hebrew name for Saturn's personification is Yahweh also known as Baal. In some contexts, the Hebrew words adon ("Lord") and Adonai ("My Lord"), which were still used as aliases for the Lord of Israel, Yahweh, were used interchangeably with the title Baal. The constructs of control are ruled by Saturn, such as government, media, education, and entertainment. Saturn is also known as the planet of karma because of its propensity for destruction and death. In astrology, it is also referred to as the planet of rules, restrictions, and limitations. The elites and world influencers worship Saturn, as their "time" lord, under Saturn's confines, which allows free energy to be consumed while humanity is conditioned.

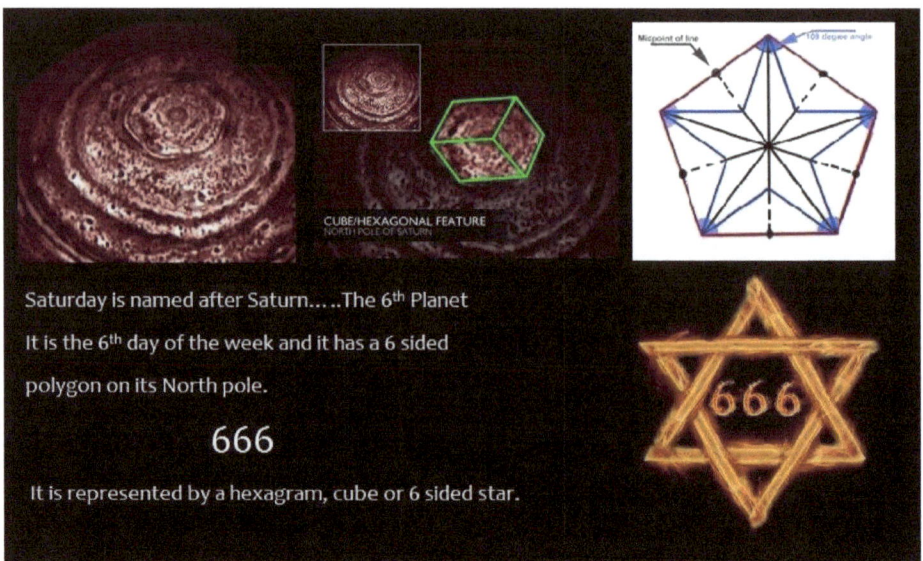

The official number for Saturn is "666," which is also the number of the beast depicted in the Book of Revelation in verse 18 of chapter 13. The connection to the number of the beast is also linked to the gods of Saturn, like Cronus, and Satan, otherly known as the devil or the beast.

Saturn has also been linked to Satan for a number of reasons. Since Saturn is the celestial body that receives the least divine light from the Sun, it is associated with the icy nature of the evil principle. In ancient paganism, Saturn was represented by the horned deity known as the "great god Pan." The creature that looks like a man and a goat is thought to be the ancestor of the Satan we see today.

"Pan was a composite creature, the upper part–with the exception of his horns–being human, and the lower part in the form of a goat. (…) The pipes of Pan signify the natural harmony of the spheres, and the god himself is a symbol of Saturn because this planet is enthroned in Capricorn, whose emblem is a goat." – **Manly P. Hall, Secret Teachings of All Ages**

The Fraternitas Saturni (FS), also known as the Brotherhood of Saturn, is recognised for carrying out sex-magical rituals more towards the Satanic arts and pagan rites. In the modern Western occult revival, the FS was the most outspoken Luciferian organization, and its sexual occultism practice may have been the most intricate of any lodge of its kind. In the FS organization, sexual occultism, Freemasonic principles, astrological cosmology, and Neo-Gnostic daemonology are all combined.

The god Saturn was referred to as "El" by Semitic civilizations. A black cube represented the supreme deity. We can find instances of the cube across the world.

Ancient Hebrews used the six-pointed star to represent Saturn; it eventually became known as the Star of David and had many additional occult connotations. The symbol is still present on Israel's flag.

The black cube-shaped Tefillin symbolises the planet Saturn in its devotion. Saturn is the hidden god of Judaism

Isis, Ra, and EL and Israel Connection

1. **ISIS:** In Egyptian mythology, Isis is considered Saturn's eldest daughter

- "I am Isis, Queen of this country. I was instructed by Mercury. No one can destroy the laws which I have established. I am the eldest daughter of Saturn, most ancient of the Gods." Quoted by **- Albert Pike**

2. **Ra:** Ra is the god to be associated with Saturn

- Inspired by Immanuel Velikovsky's work, David Talbot attempted to identify some of the motifs behind Roman Saturn worship in his 1980 book The Saturn Myth. "A Greek ostracon cited by the eminent classicist Franz Boll identifies the Egyptian Sun god Ra, not with our Sun, but with Saturn." — **David Talbot (1980), The Saturn Myth**
- Saturn's Greek equivalent is believed to be Cronus. It's unclear if the Egyptian god Ra is equivalent to Cronus or Saturn, depending on the context; One perspective is as follows:

"The first man, according to the Egyptians, was Hephaestus [Ptah], who was the inventor of fire. From him descended the Sun. After whom Agathodaemon. After whom Cronus [Saturn]. Then Osiris. And then Typhon [Set], the brother of Osiris. After whom was Orus [Horus], the son of Osiris and Isis. These were the first Egyptian kings. After them, the empire descended by a long succession to Bites, through a lapse of 13,900 years [months]; reckoned, I say, in lunar years of thirty days to each: for even now, they call the month a year. After the gods, a race of demi-gods reigned 1,255 years. Then reigned other kings 1,817 years. After them, thirty Memphite kings, 1,790 years. Than ten Thynite kings, 330 years. Then came the kingdom of the manes and demi-gods. 5,813. The number of years altogether amounts to 11,000; which also are lunar years, that is to say, months. All the lunar years which the Egyptians allow to the reigns of the gods, the demi-gods, and the Manes, are 24,900." — **Eusebius (300AD), Publication Family Magazine: Or Monthly Abstract of General Knowledge, Volume 1**

3. **EL:** The Phoenicians regarded El/Saturn as their chief deity; Eusebius informs us that El, a name used also in the Bible as a name for God, was the name of Saturn.

"It was a custom of the ancients in great crises of danger for the rulers of a city or nation, in order to avert the common ruin, to give up the most beloved of their children for sacrifice as a ransom to avenging daemons; and those who were thus ongoing sacrificed with mystic rites. Cronus then, whom the Phoenicians call Elus (EL), who was king of the country and subsequently, after his decease, was deified as the star SATURN, had by a nymph of the country named Anobret an only begotten son, whom they on this account called Iedud, the only begotten being still so called among the Phoenicians; and when very great dangers from war had beset the country, he arrayed his son in royal apparel, and prepared an altar, and sacrificed him." - **Immanuel Velikovsky**

- El is called again and again, Toru El ("Bull El or the Bull God"). He is Batnyu Binwati ("creator of creatures") Abu Ban eli ("father of the gods"), and Abu Adami ("father of man").
- El is a generic word for the God that could be used for any god including Baal, Molech, or Yahweh.

"….Cronus then, whom the Phoenicians call Elus (EL), who was king of the country and subsequently, after his decease, was deified as the star of SATURN, had by a nymph of the country named Anobret an ONLY BEGOTTEN SON whom they on this account called "IEOUD" the only begotten being still so called among the Phoenicians and when very great dangers from war had beset the country he arrayed his son in royal apparel, and prepared an altar and SACRIFICED HIM….." - **Bishop Eusebius; Praeparatio Evangelica (I. chs ix-x)**

Conclusion: Is-Ra-El is a combination of the names of the pagan god's Isis, Ra, and El, which I am able to confirm. Each of these three pagan deities is associated with Saturn. Additionally, both the Israeli symbol and the Tefillin (black cube) represent Saturn.

The Christ Cube

In Semitic civilisations, the supreme deity El, also referred to as Saturn, was symbolised by a black cube. We can find instances of the cube across the world such as in the formation of the cross. The cross is an unfolded cube which is seen in the six squares of the symbol.

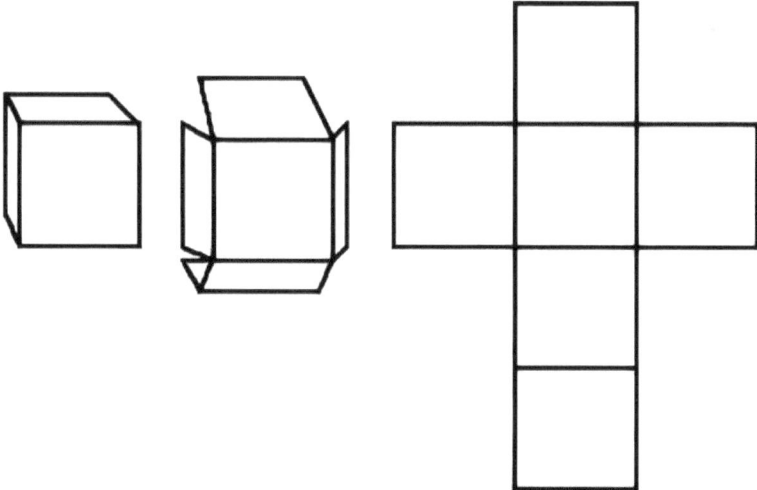

Pope JohnXXIII says: "…the heavenly Church, already have the CUBE within their heart. The CUBE is the sign of membership, and it cannot be gainsaid: you either have the CUBE or you do not. It is the mark of the Godhead... Jesus has shown me the CUBE in the heart. It lights up. It is a crystal. It is a perfect CUBE!"

For Christians, "The Lord of the Sabbath" is really Yehushua/Jesus, and a cube is a symbol of perfection. While the depth and height are vertical, the breadth and length are horizontal. These are the aspects of Christ that we must face. A CUBE is made up of these measurements and is solid, robust, sturdy, unbreakable, and immovable. Together with the saints, we must comprehend the scope of this enormous, all-encompassing CUBE-Christ. According to Freemasonry, the cube symbolises fraternal perfection

- "The city was laid out like a square, as long as it was wide. He measured the city with the rod and found it to be 12,000 stadia in length, and as wide and high as it is long." - **Revelation 21:16**

This indicates that it has a cube-like form. The height, width, and length are all the same. The city is 12,000 furlongs in size. A mile is eight furlongs long. This city's dimensions are 1500 miles long, 1500 miles wide, and 1500 miles high (In basic numerology, 1,500 Miles = 6, 1,500 Miles = 6, 1,500 Miles = 6). Heaven resembles a cube with four squares. The measures are astrological, which is fortunate for them. With a length, width, and height of 12,000 furlongs apiece, the New Jerusalem, the city of Heaven described in Revelation, is a perfect cube. The cube has 12 edges, each of which is 12,000 furlongs long. Additionally, the 12 zodiac signs that control the 12 borders of the Cube of Space are a reference to the 12 gates, as well.

Saturn and EL

Saturn was referred to as 'El.' The elevation of the term 'El' could be used in the etymology of words: such as 'El-der' - from worshiping 'El,' then you get 'El-ections' to become an 'El-der,' and then you get 'El-ite' to be known as superior.

Black has long been associated with Saturn and Saturnian worship in the realm of the occult. People who have attained the highest degree of indoctrination actually honor Saturn, the god Cube, by donning the pileo, the graduate's cap, and dressing in full black.

Rings are also attributed to Saturn, in fact, the implementation of such accessories like wedding rings or jewelry rings are paganistic in origin. Hieroglyphs on a tomb painting found in one of Egypt's tombs, which date back to 2200 BC, provide some of our earliest evidence for marriage ceremonies. Roman marriage ceremonies also included the exchange of rings as part of the ritual. In the Celtic myths, Saturn, also known as Lord of the Rings, appears to be the reason why people still exchange wedding rings to seal a wedding or to represent a ring (or disk, if we refer to the Sun) behind images of saints and pious people (haloes) or ancient Celtic crosses.

Courts and Saturn

All courts are housed inside prisms, which are quadrangular structures designed to hold or encase people, which are energy bodies. A judge will be the figure of authority in the room under this type of event.

The judge who presides the ruling of the court represents Saturn by wearing all black to honour its highest form. The court is then ruled by time, Saturn being the "father of time" in the ancient past. Because of its power of judging, the court also imposes punishments; this serves as a reminder that Saturn, the planet of Karma, is responsible for death and propensity. It is frequently referred to as the planet of rules, restrictions, and limitations in astrology.

The bench, which derives from the late Latin word for bank, is where the judge is seated. Consequently, the court makes decisions that benefit the bank. Again reaffirming Saturn's archontic principle, materialism is the planet's primary feature. Under Saturn's confines, the main ones (people in charge) will receive payment regardless of who wins or loses. As such, the judge makes decisions on behalf of the bank. In court, it's like a game of tennis, which simulates the back and forth clattering (clattering; root imitative for racket) of opposing sides.

Chapter 8: Lunar Cults - Adoration or Veneration of the Moon

Legacy of Moses

Moses is shown with horns in sculptures, paintings, and drawings. It has been shown everywhere around the world. People have questioned why Moses has horns? Moreover, it is intriguing to understand the importance of Moses' horns. Sin was the name given to the Moon-god in the ancient Mesopotamian religion. Additionally, the lowest quarter of the Moon was always used to symbolise him. As a result, Moon worship was symbolised by the lowest quarter of the Moon. Given that the Native Americans numbered their days by the number of Moons, they too have horns. They lived in times similar to those of the Hebrews. The Native Americans experienced the same trend after six o'clock, when a new day began.

Lunar simply means the Moon, and all of these peoples—from the ancient Hebrews to the Native Americans—were utilising a lunar calendar. Thus, the bull's horns served as the lunar sign. These are the horns that Moses wore in Israel, and they represent the lunar symbol that is seen in many different religions. The Moon is shown in Egyptian art, and you will notice sculptures of arms lifted to honour and adore the Moon. In Christianity, the blessed mother sits above the Moon. The Moon was a commonplace in the ancient religious world, showing us how significant it was even in the time of Moses. Moon worship was widespread in Egypt and remains prevalent in the Islamic world today.

Moses Depicted With Horns Across The World

The Moon-god Sin is a well-known example from the ancient world. Additionally, Ai was a mountain in the ancient world, particularly in ancient Egypt. Thus, when you combine the Moon-god Sin and the mountain Ai, you get Sinai, or Mount Sinai. "Sin" (meaning "the Moon" or "to shine") is the term for the Moon, and it is part of the name of Sinai. The Moon-cult was established in the peninsula as early as Egypt's pre-dynastic period. The southern Sinai peninsula appears to have been the primary location of Moon worship when it was taken from the Semitic people by the Egyptians, who had established temples and mining camps there.

Today, Mount Sinai is regarded as the epicenter and the actual beginning of the Jewish faith as it expanded over the Middle East. Interestingly, the term synagogue is spelt SIN in Israel, even though it was originally spelt SYN throughout most of the western world. In Israel, it is spelt SIN-agogue because of the Moon-god Sin. Since Sin was the Moon-god, the synagogue essentially means temple of the Moon.

In the majority of the western world, the term synagogue was originally spelt SYN, however in Israel, it is spelt SIN.

The Moon was highly respected in the ancient Arabic world; this is likely due to several events created by the new Moon, as the Arabic and ancient worlds realised how much the Moon affected human beings. The Moon was crucial to the ancient world since it affects our food supply and pulls the Earth's waters. Their days began at six o'clock, at sundown, therefore they always counted the days using the Moon.

Moon Worship in Islam

In the Kaaba, Muhammad was raised worshipping a variety of pagan gods, including Allah and the Moon, also known as Hubal. Muhammad ceased worshipping the Moon once he became a monotheist as a result of Christian (Catholic) influence. For all Muslims from that time till now, the same holds true. Nonetheless, the crescent Moon serves as Islam's worldwide symbol. Muslims will contend that the crescent Moon symbol wasn't used in Islam for the first several centuries following Muhammad, and that archaeological evidence does not support this claim. However, Muslims also assert that the Koran was complete when Muhammad lived, but there is no archaeological support for this assertion either. We could be certain that the crescent Moon symbol has been used in Pre-Islamic Arabia, and that Moon worship was more common in Arabia than anywhere else in the world. The belief that there is no historical relationship between Islam and the crescent Moon symbol, which is a pagan Moon deity worship symbol, is a fabrication of history. The crescent Moon symbol is still used on the flags and on mosques in the majority of Arab and Muslim nations.

In the Middle East, archaeologists have discovered temples dedicated to the Moon-god. In ancient times, the Moon-god was the most widely practiced religion, from the highlands of Turkey to the banks of the Nile. The Sumerians, the earliest literary civilisation, provided us with thousands of clay tablets that detailed their religious beliefs. In ancient Mesopotamia, the most common religion was the worship of the Moon-god. As their preferred name for the Moon-god, the Assyrians, Babylonians, and Akkadians changed the term Suen to the word Sin.

The Moon in its crescent phase was typically used to symbolise the Moon-god Sin in ancient Syria and Canna. To highlight each of the Moon's phases, the full Moon was occasionally positioned inside the crescent Moon. The stars were the daughters of Sin's wife, the Sun-goddess. In this case, Ishtar was a daughter of Sin. Sacrifices to the Moon-god are described in the Pas Shamra scriptures. The Moon-god was occasionally referred to as Kusuh in the Ugaritic writings. He is portrayed on statue heads and on wall murals in Egypt and Persia. He judged both humanity and the gods. The Moon-god was often the focus of Israel's worship. In reality, the crescent Moon symbol appears on seal imprints, steles, ceramics, amulets, clay tablets, cylinders, weights, necklaces, earrings, wall paintings, and more across the ancient world. A copper calf with a crescent Moon on its forehead was discovered at Tell-el-Obeid. A crescent Moon is inlaid with shells on the forehead of an idol that has a bull's body and a man's head. Since the Moon-god was the head of the gods, the crescent symbol is situated at the top of the register of gods in Ur's Stele of Ur-Nammu. In homage to the Moon-god, even bread was cooked in the shape of a crescent. In tablets from that era, the Ur of the Chaldees was frequently referred to as Nannar because of its intense devotion to the Moon-god.

Evidence collected from both North and South Arabia indicates that worship of the Moon-god was still the most common cult throughout Muhammad's lifetime. Several inscriptions state that the Moon-god was known as Sin, but his title was al-ilah, which means "the deity," indicating that he was the highest or leader of the gods. In pre-Islamic times, the Moon-god was known as al-ilah, meaning the god, which was abbreviated to Allah. The pagan Arabs even gave their children names that referenced Allah. For instance, Allah was a component of the names of Muhammad's father and uncle. Even in Muhammad's day, Allah was a name for the Moon-god, as evidenced by the names their pagan parents gave them.

Muhammad was brought up in the faith of Allah, the Moon-god. However, he went beyond what his fellow pagan Arabs had done. Muhammad concluded that Allah was not only the greatest god but also the only god, despite their belief that Allah, also known as the Moon-god, was the greatest of all gods and the highest deity among a pantheon of deities. There is no denying that Allah was a pagan deity before the advent of Islam, especially now that we have the real idols of the Moon-god.

Origin of The Name Allah

Does this make it any wonder that the crescent Moon is an image of Islam? That their minarets and mosques have a crescent Moon on top of them? That the flags of Islamic countries include a crescent Moon? Why does the crescent Moon's appearance in the sky mark the start and finish of the month during which Muslims fast? By introducing people to familiarised beliefs and concepts, Islam's founders blended pagan beliefs into their creation in an effort to win acceptance from the masses.

The Arabic compound word al-ilah is where the term "Allah" originates. "The" is the definite article "al," while "god" is the Arabic word for "the god," ilah. We can see right once that (a) this is a generic name rather than a proper one, similar to the Hebrew El, which, as we have shown, was used for any deity; and (b) Allah is an Arabic word, not a foreign one, as it would have been if it had been taken from the Hebrew Bible. Also, as "Allah" is an Arabic name that is only used to refer to an Arabic god, it would be incorrect to compare it to the Hebrew or Greek words for God (El and Theos). Thus, according to the Encyclopaedia of Religion, "'Allah' is a pre-Islamic name... corresponding to the Babylonian Bel" (ed. James Hastings, Edinburgh, T. & T. Clark, 1908, I:326).

Main Pre Islamic Moon God's in Arabia

Sin: Sîn is a Semitic Moon-god who was worshipped in ancient Middle Eastern faiths. Sin was one of the most important gods in the Assyrian and Babylonian pantheons, he ruled over knowledge and the calendar. His primary sites of devotion were Ur, where he was known as Nanna, and Harran. The crescent Moon served as Sin's symbol. It is evident that this was the most common religion in Sumeria based on the quantity of artefacts pertaining to its devotion. In ancient Mesopotamia, the most common religion was the worship of the Moon-god. As their preferred name for this deity, the Assyrians, Babylonians, and Arkkadians changed the word Suen to Sîn.

Impression of the cylinder seal of Ḥašḫamer, a high priest of Sîn, ca. 2100 B.C.E.

Hubal: In pre-Islamic Arabia, Hubal was a god worshipped by the Quraysh at the Kaaba in Mecca, according to Arabian mythology. The human figure that served as the god's icon was thought to be in charge of divination, which was done by throwing arrows in front of the statue. The Sira has accounts of Meccan pagans standing next to the image of Hubal and praying to Allah. Arabs, addressing Hubal as Allah, stood next to him and offered prayers. When Muhammad arrived and destroyed the idol of Hubal, the Arabs were left without an idol of Allah to worship and Hubal was forgotten.

 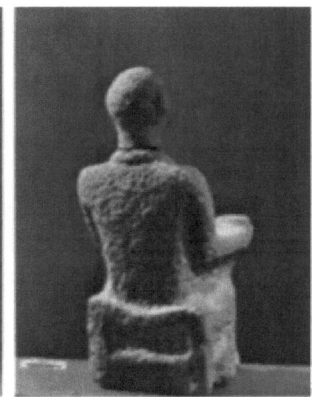

Statue from Tel Hazor, used to link to lunar diety Hubal

Harran, City of the Moon-God: The Moon-god, also known as Sin, was the patron deity of Harran, a city near the northernmost tip of the Sumerian Empire. Harran carried on the developing practice of worshipping the Moon-god from around 2000 BC to 1200 AD. Harran, Sheba, and other cities were traders "in blue clothes and broidered work, in chests of rich apparel, bound with cords and made of cedar," according to Ezekiel 27:23. Exaggerated stories of sacrifice that are most likely untrue are a common feature of Christian and Muslim accounts of Harran. However, since the bull was at Ur, a garlanded black bull was slain in public. According to Moslem accounts, Ta'uz was celebrated with seasonal weeping at Harran and among Bedouin in the desert as late as the tenth century.

Star and Crescent of Harran Coin

Karum: Known as Karum, the Assyrians had founded 20 separate trading colonies across Anatolia. It is possible to argue that the Assyrians created the most advanced commerce system of their era.

Anatolian mural from Karum - notice the boxed pre-Islamic Crescent-and-Star glyph

Yerah: A major temple dedicated to the Moon-god was unearthed at Hazor, Palestine, in the 1950s. Two Moon-god idols were discovered. A figure of a man seated on a throne with a crescent Moon carved into his breast was featured in each (see below left). It is evident from the accompanying inscriptions that these were Moon-god idols. Arms are extended towards the Moon-god, who is symbolised by the full Moon inside the crescent Moon, according to the worship tablet discovered at the same location. A number of smaller sculptures that were recognised as the daughters of the Moon-god by their inscriptions were also discovered.

Al-Lat, Al-Uzza, and Manat: In northern Arabia, thousands of inscriptions have also been gathered from rocks and walls. Additionally, votive bowls and reliefs used in worship of the "daughters of Allah" have been found. A crescent Moon over the three daughters, Al-Lat, Al-Uzza, and Manat, is sometimes used to symbolise Allah the Moon-god. Archaeological discoveries in North Arabia pertaining to Al-Lat are covered in. With three daughters, the main god in Mecca was called Allah. Al-uzzah, Almanat, and Allat. According to their traditions, they served as intercessors for Allah. In pre-Islamic Arabia, the goddesses Aluzza, Allat, and Almanat were a trinity. Al-uzza was associated with Aphrodite, Almanat with Nemesis, and Allat with the goddess Athena. Before the advent of Islam, Allah was considered a general "sky god," and the concept of divinity itself was connected to the name Allah. Muhammad was born to pagan parents, which is an undeniable fact. Both his mother, Amina, and father, Abdullah, were heathens and worshiped several idols. He was immersed in paganism throughout his whole youth, most likely until he was a teenager. Muhammad transformed the idols into "The Daughters of Allah" and made the God of the Koran out of Hubal, the highest of the 360 gods worshipped by the Quraysh tribe in the Kabbah. All three of Al'lat's incarnations were influenced by the Banat, who represented Light, Rain, and Earth and were the three daughters of Baal, the Canaanite deity.

2nd century AD relief from Hatra depicting the 3 goddesses

The Black Cube in Mecca - Saturn

The Kaaba, in the Saudi Arabian holy city of Mecca, is an example of Saturnian veneration in the Islamic religion. The black cube of Saturn is depicted within a Masonic circle at Mecca.

Millions and millions of people each year congregate around Saturn's black cube, giving the dark overlords their energy. Saturn = Black Square, Black Cube, and Black Sun. All used sacred geometry to make Saturn's worship stronger. Every year an abundance of people walk around the Kaaba in Mecca, unknowingly giving their energy to Saturn. Additionally, making the trip to Mecca always faces the Sun. The Kaaba, the pagan monument, has had its share of history in astrological reverence in early Islam. The Kaaba of Mecca is the old shrine of the 360 pagan gods and goddesses that were worshiped. All Abrahamic religions are in fact all pagan in their core and have created a wide share of global trauma including mass murders, wars, and division.

Every Arab household had its own god, and the Kaaba was encircled by 360 idols prior to Muhammad's arrival. In addition, Arabs believed in a vague god with many offsprings and jinn. The main deities of the pre-Islamic era included the Moon-god, Hubal, whose worship was associated with the Black Stone of the Kaaba; al-Lat ("the Goddess"), who was worshipped as a square stone; al-Uzzah ("the Mighty"), who was associated with the morning star and was worshipped as a granite slab shaped like a thigh bone between al Talf and Mecca; and Manat, the goddess of destiny, who was worshipped as a black stone on the road between Mecca and Medina. The stones were believed to symbolise cosmic powers and to have fallen from the Sun, Moon, stars, and planets. The Black Stone, which Muslims pray in the direction today, is really the colour of burned umber. Long before Muhammad, their ancestors worshipped it and thought it sprang from the Moon. The stone has never been the subject of a scientific inquiry. An Iraqi sect of Qarmatians removed and broke the stone in 930, but the fragments were eventually given back. Pitch-sealed and secured with silver wire, the sections are several feet high and around 10 inches in diameter overall; they are now revered in patched-together condition.

It must be said that Catholicism, Judaism and Islam all appear to have preserved in their traditions not only fragments of the cult of Saturn but also of the Sun, and Moon. Over fifteen prehistoric religions existed before our three main modern-day religions, and all of them share the same ideas from the past. Modern religion has incorporated pagan beliefs in order to persuade people during those times to accept it by exposing them to familiarized concepts and pagan practices. It is now time for people to really question who they really worship.

Chapter 9: Islam's Relationship With the Vatican and the Occult

Muslims in Templar Membership - Historical Fact

In order to carry out the vile tasks of the Vatican, Muslims were in the Knights Templar. All of this was done so that Rome can eliminate anyone who disagrees with the Pope. It didn't matter if they used Christians and Muslims. As a covert service for the Pope, the Knights Templar were finally wiped out since they weren't actually pursuing the Pope's long-term goals. To take over the Middle East, the Catholic Church used Muslims.

Authentically, the original Knights Templar rejected the idea of the "Crusades" as supposedly being to eliminate Muslims or eradicate Islam. This historical fact is proven by the Temple Rule of 1129 AD, in which the Templar Order criticized that the Crusades "did not do what it should, that is to defend ....but strove to plunder, deposit or kill" (Rule 2). It clearly specified that the only real purpose of Templar warfare was to "remove from the land enemies of Christ," "not kill Muslims" (Rule 14). And the original Latin says only to "strike" enemies, proving no specific intent to kill (Rule 57). Quite contrary to polarized misconceptions the Templars fully understood that Muslims were not necessarily enemies, that the "real enemies of Christ" could even be evil doers pretending to be Christians and that the "enemies of Christ" were generally the same as the enemies of Islam. Indeed, evil doers are essentially the enemies of all faith, opposed to the principle of religion itself and are thus the enemies of God.

Therefore the Templars were never "Crusaders" against Muslims, and did not agree with any such philosophy. Rather, the Knights Templar were warrior-monks fighting for good against evil, regardless of which religions may or may not be involved.

The most conclusive evidence that Mulsims were in fact accepted in membership in the Templar Order was codified in the Temple Rule of 1129 AD, which was expanded by the later "Hierarchical Rules" added from ca. 1150-1250 AD: One key amendment (ca. 1200 AD), specifically provides: "If a brother goes out from the house and... enters into another religion, it would do no harm if he returns to rejoin the house; but he… will not be held by anything... to that religion nor to us also, for he has returned from the one and from the other." (Rule 630) [2]

The Vatican Islam Connection

The similarities between the rise of Islam and the Roman Catholic Church, both of which adopted pagan concepts in an effort to win converts, are what individually amaze me the most. Muhammad was not the only religious figure to plagiarise other religions. Phoney "Christian" churches have also engaged in this kind of conduct.

According to the Encyclopedia of Religion, the Babylonian Bell's pre-Islamic equivalent is Allah. Thus, the deity in this ancient pagan religion is Baal. On page 451 of Morals and Dogma, we read AL-DE-BARAN, which translates to "the foremost or leading star" in Arabic, could only have earned that title if it preceded or led everyone else. The year therefore began with the Sun in Taurus with several antique paintings from Egypt and Assyria depicting a bull with crescent or lunette horns and the Sun's disc between them. When the year began with Sol (the Sun) and Luna (the I in Taurus), there was a celebration of the first new Moon festival everywhere. This was a straight illusion to the big festival of the year. The conjunctive Sun and Moon are always represented by the desk and the crescent. In essence, that refers to the masculine and feminine aspects of the god. We could see the eye (the eye of Osiris), the horn, and the disc in the horn, which symbolised the Sun god's descent into the mother's womb to be carried by Isis. It was worship of the Celestial Cow Mehet-weret. The Moon (the sickle Moon) is therefore symbolised by the horns.

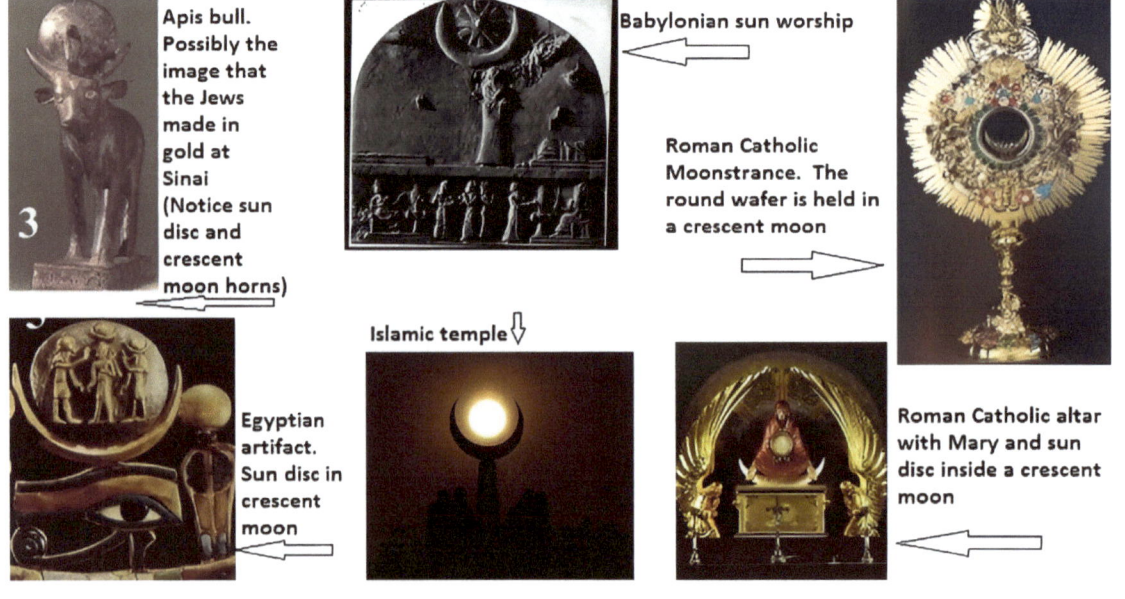

The half Moon with the solar disc within and the baal-hadad (the birth of the Sun) are features of older religions from Babylon itself that are Assyrian in form. The ancient symbol of Baal, which was found in Mesopotamia, was identical to the half Moon and the star that symbolised the male and female aspects of the Sun's birth (Isis and Osiris). This would be the masculine and female Isis and Horus or Ashtharoth and Thamus. As we've already spoken about, the Egyptian is the same. Baal worship is what this is. The fold is both masculine and feminine. Since the pope now serves as the spokesperson for the Babylonian religion, the papacy has the exact same function. Therefore, he has a circular wafer disc that represents Baal when he speaks the mass, and it is nace in a monstrance, which is a hat Moon, after a mass. Consequently, the Sun's birth might be represented by this fold. In another monstrance, the host is positioned to symbolise the Sun's birth.

Therefore, a half Moon with a star or Sun inside is used as a symbol in Catholicism. This fascinating clock may be seen within a Roman Catholic church in Germany. Every hour of the day, they attempt to take images of the Moon, the star, and this particular star, which has eight points. As the clock rotates, the Sun god (baal-hadad) is born every time the long and short arms intercalate.

The symbol of a half Moon with a star or Sun inside is used in Catholicism.

The Sun, which was an icon of Sun worship, and the cross, which is obviously a symbol of the Sun god, are both evident if we examine the symbolism on the outside of the Catholic Cathedral. The magnificent Abdullah Mosque, one of the best, was constructed by King Abdullah and is located across the street. The Sun's symbols are displayed on the gates. Same religion, same symbols. Additionally, the Moon—the sickle Moon—that was shown on the Catholic Church's clock is shown here. It served as Baal's symbol.

Abdullah Mosque Moon Crescent

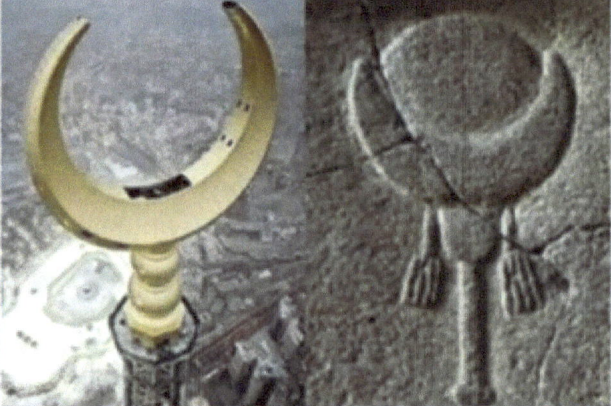
Crescent Moon in Mecca & Crescent Pagan Carving Representing Baal-Hadad

Freemasonry's Usage of Islam

The 29 degrees of the Scottish Rite are comparable to the York Rite, and advancement along this line leads to the degrees known as "Knights Templar." Additionally, 32nd Degree Masons and Knights Templar who want to participate can join the Shrine (Ancient Arabic Order, Nobles of the Mystic Shrines).Therefore, those of the greatest rank can become Shrines. The Arabic Order is in effect at the Shrine.

"The Shrine (Ancient Arabic Order, Nobles of the Mystic Shrine) Page. 73... The Shrine, the "Show Army of Masonry." maintains a very high profile... it is necessary to be a 32nd Degree Mason for six months before being eligible to join the Shrine."

Joining the Shriners is exclusive to the top Freemasons. In addition, all of the well-known Americans march in Little New York as the Shriners. The Shrine is in the name of Allah. The Koran is placed on the altar at the shrine by the so-called Christians of the 32nd degree, who are now aware that they worship Lucifer. Now that the Bibles are gone, you become a Shriner when you reach the pinnacle of Freemasonry. They now take a solemn oath to subject themselves to the dreadful penalties of Masonry:

"I do hereby, upon this Bible, and on the mysterious legend of the Koran, and its dedication to the Mohammedan faith, promise and swear and vow … that I will never reveal any secret part or portion whatsoever of the ceremonies … and now upon this sacred book, by the sincerity of a Moslem's oath I here register this irrevocable vow … in willful violation whereof may I incur the fearful penalty of having my eyeballs pierced to the center with a three-edged blade, my feet flayed and I be forced to walk the hot sands upon the sterile shores of the Red Sea until the flaming Sun shall strike me with livid plague, and may Allah, the god of Arab, Moslem and Mohammedan, the god of our fathers, support me to the entire fulfillment of the same. Amen. Amen. Amen."

Can a Christian be a Shriner? "No" is the answer. A candidate swears allegiance to the Koran, not to a Bible. The truth is that Freemasonry incorporates elements of all three major Abrahamic religions into its rituals and goal for a new global order. According to Christian doctrine, a Christian cannot equally become a Freemason. After earning his Third Degree, the Master Mason is granted eternal life, and after earning his Royal Arch Degree, he is referred to as "A Christ." When the Shriner makes his Mystic Shrine pledge, he unquestionably and completely commits to Islam.

What is the reason behind the use of religion as a new global order today? The reason for this is because it divides people and manipulates their view to continue depending on a fictitious saviour. They can manipulate people with fear and false hope to a greater extent the more religion they can indoctrinate us with. Albert Pike, the Godfather of Freemasonry, acknowledges this openly. In a letter to Giussepe Mazzini in 1871, he reportedly writes: **"The Third World War"** must be fomented by taking advantage of the differences caused by the "agentur" of the "Illuminati" between the political Zionists and the leaders of Islamic World. The war must be conducted in such a way that Islam (the Moslem Arabic World) and political Zionism (the State of Israel) mutually destroy each other.

Whether or not the statement is true, it is clear that the churches, mosques, cathedrals, and even some of the organisations that the Masonic order has constructed are crucial to Freemasonry's influence on religion today. Freemason Joseph Smith formed the Mormon Church, Freemason Charles Taze Russell founded the Jehovah Witnesses, and the founders of the Seventh Day Adventists were also covertly Masons, if not inspired by Masonry. In addition, there are several religious Masonic organisations that are part of the York Rite cults, which were established by Masons. How many religious people from different backgrounds do you believe this Masonic order has consumed? Well, there are many who are clueless and who associate with this fraternity in a way that contradicts their own beliefs.

Nothing has changed in the world since then; religious violence from the past still occurs today because its fundamental purpose is deception. Religion and the stories that people have written in the name of "God" are completely unconnected to God. God is consciousness—not the creator, but the very source of creation itself. You separate yourself from the source, and you immediately become a limited being if you believe that "God" is something outside of yourself. You and everyone else are made up of this force, divine energy, and frequency. When you embrace the god (deity) that has been assigned to you by religious dogma, you become their spiritual prisoner.

Pope John Paul II kissing the Koran within the Church (1999)

Chapter 10: Legends, Myths, and Origins

Chi Rho = Saturnian Symbolism

Christ, whose name in Greek starts with the letter X, is occasionally represented by the diagonal cross. In ancient Greek mythology, it also stood for the number 1,000. In Roman mythology, it even symbolised Chronos, the god of time, the planet Saturn, and the god Saturn. We are also informed that the Chi Rho was the monogram of Osiris in Egypt, as the Sun was known at Abydos, or that it was a sign of Jupiter Ammon, who was also the Sun.

The Greeks also used the letter chi as a solar symbol, and they associated it with Saturn as the abbreviation of his name, Chronos, which is a wheel-shaped sign made up of the first two letters combined, or "Chi-Rho." As the initials of Christ, both abbreviations were accepted by Christians and are still in use today, with the chi showing up in our abbreviation for Christmas, Xmas. One of the most well-known Christian symbols is the bind-letters, or monogram, Chi-Rho, which is found in practically every Roman Catholic church.

The enormous, imposingly drawn single S in the Pompeian Graffiti might have stood for Saturnus or possibly Sol, just as the Chi could have stood for Chronus. Despite what has been thought so far, it was not an abbreviation for salutem. Saturnus-Aion, the god of SATOR, could have been PATER NOSTER since the solar cross, represented by an X or a +, was his symbol.

The following are monograms of Osiris.. They are also Jupiter Ammon's monograms. This figure can be found on one of Decius's coins, which has the phrase BAPATO. Decius was the great persecutor of the Christians. In the same way, this word appears on the staffs of Osiris and Isis. The cross of Constantine was nothing more than the Chi-Rho, the monogram of Osiris, and afterwards of Christ.

Origins of Abraham, Isaac, and Jacob

Abraham, also known as Ab-Ra-Ham (father Ra of Egypt), the fabled eleventh descendant of Noah (or Nun), is the anthropomorphism of the "Father Ra born of Nun," or Ra (fire), born out of land or keme (Earth) that arose after the flood (water), according to the Judeo-Christian-Islamic creation account.

In short, Abraham is not a real person; rather, he is the Sun god (Sun) that emerged from the pyramid, a land mound that formed following the yearly 150-day Nile flood. This entity is part of the creation myth of Heliopolis in Egyptology (2800 BC), which is technically a syncretism of the supreme god-entity of the creation myths of Heliopolis, Hermopolis, Memphis, and Thebes. In Hinduism, Abraham was also reconceived as the creator god Brahma.

The relationship between the Hindu creator god Brahma and the Jewish, Christian, and Islamic patriarch Abraham is one of the more important unifying decipherments. These parallels occur in at least six ways:

1. The primary creator god of the Egyptian pantheon, Ra, is credited with creating all people, along with Abraham and Brahma.
2. "Father Ra son of Nun" is the etymology shared by Abraham and Brahma (water-fire-Earth theory).
3. Both Abraham and Brahma derived from the Nun (Noah and Ma-Nu, respectively).
4. Sarai and Saraswati, the namesakes of Abraham and Brahma, respectively, are the same sister-wife.
5. The sister-wife parable (creation by incest rewrite) is shared by Abraham and Brahma.
6. The slaying of son reoccurs in both cases (release of the soul rewrite / Osiris-Horus splitting rewrite).

The fact that chemistry and Abraham (or Brahma) share the same root etymology (see: chemistry etymology) is not a coincidence, since both represent different belief systems that explain how humans evolved from the Earth's elements heated by the Sun on a cyclical basis:

Name	Etymology
Abraham | Brahma	Father "Ra" born of the "Nun" (pyramid) – or kÄ"me, pronounced: 'chem' (Greenberg, 1996), the name of the black fertile soil left behind following the receding of the annual 150-day Nile flood.
Chemistry	From Coptic word for "Egypt", *kÄ"me* (pronounced: chem) or *chÄ"mia*, according Plutarch (*On Isis and Osiris*, 100AD), named as such owing to the black color of its soil; hence the synonym "black art" (Partington, 1936).

The Hebrew pronunciation of Noah's second son's name, Ham, is "Chem." He is portrayed as the father of the Egyptian and African peoples. The name comes from the old Egyptian name for Egypt, "Keme." It alludes to the rich black soil that remains after the yearly Nile flood recedes to its banks and is known as "the black land."

Human Chemical Thermodynamics

To put it briefly, Abraham and chemistry both explain how humans came to be by pointing to a relationship between the Sun (or heat) and "Chem," or "arisen land" (fertile soil), or Sun birth after the flood in the former case, or 92 naturally occurring "elements" of the periodic table that were heated by the Sun on a cyclical basis in the latter case, which is explained by synthesis/analysis and chemical thermodynamics.

Consequently, it would be determined to be made up of the alphabet's initial two letters. The Hebrew word for father, AB, contains precisely this. Connecting it to the Egyptian RA, the fiery Sun god, we get AB-RA-M, which eventually developed the advanced heavenly powers symbolised by the fifth Hebrew letter, he, to become AB-RA-H-AM. Furthermore, it is little a coincidence that even UR starts with the letter U, which (together with V) stands for the downward line of descent, the turning upward, and the return to the heights, as Abram emerged from the primordial empyreal fire, UR. Not only is there no evidence that a person like Abraham ever existed, but archaeologists additionally believe that, given what we now know about the ancient Israelite beginnings, such a person could not have been.

Origins of Church

Nowadays, the word "church" is a transliteration of the Greek word "Ekklesia" and can be found in most English-language bibles. This is a translation error; the Greek term "Ekklesia" means "out calling," and it also refers to an "Assembly" in English, such as "a meeting" or "an out gathering." Qahal is the term that means "Congregation" or "Assembly" in Hebrew. According to ecclesiastical and other sources, the term "church" is derived from the Greek word "kuriakon," which means "house of the Lord." The New Testament does not, however, include kuriakon.

This small piece of information is crucial for a number of reasons, and because no attempt has been made to rectify the mistranslation, people have been led astray into accepting a falsehood.

When and how did the Bible adopt the word "church"? The word "Church" comes from the Saxon words "circe," "circ," or "cyric," according to a dictionary. The term "church" has its roots in pagan mythology. False gods were typically worshipped in circular structures by pagans, and circles were often used in their iconography. "Circe," a legendary witch goddess in Homer's epic poem "Odyssey," is the source of the words "circle," "circus," and "church." She employed poisons to transform men into animals. The word "church" has a pagan meaning of "a place to worship a god." Church is more than just a group of people; it's a "place." The Roman Sun God "Christos Helios," from whence the name Christ is derived, had a daughter named "Circe," a minor goddess of magic (or occasionally a nymph, witch, enchantress, or sorceress). It is clearly of Pagan origin and has nothing to do with the Most High or his people. Instead, it is entirely related to those who, in their Roman Pantheon known as the Church, worship the Sun as a god on Sundays. The majority of people in these religious establishments are unaware that in 321 AD, Roman Emperor Constantine the Great established Sunday as a day of rest honouring Helios, the Greek and Roman Sun god. Constantine was a worshipper of "Christos-Helios," or "Christ-The-True-Sun." The vast majority of churches built today are 501-C(3) corporations under state jurisdiction. A church that was established with the state's approval and so embraces the benefits that the state offers is no longer under the "headship" of Messiah; rather, it has submitted itself to the state's authority alone. Since they are entirely at the mercy of the State in all respects, 501-C(3) churches and any other church founded with state approval under any "Corporate form" will no longer be allowed to debate anything that could conflict with or go against the laws or regulations set out by the State.

Kyrios
↓
Kyriake (oikia)
↓
Kirika or kirk
↓
Cirice, circe
↓
Church

The Greek word for "church," kuriakon or kyriakon, is referred to as "kirk" in Scotland, "Kirche" in Germany, and "kerk" in the Netherlands. It refers to a structure (the home of Kurios, or the house of the Lord), where 1 Corinthians 8:5 states that there are several lords. The Pagans were known to worship Sun Gods and regard them as Lords. People nowadays are unaware that they are referring to an idol since calling the church the home of the Lord does not actually denote what the Lord is because that meaning never did. Kirche means Sun worship since it is akin to the Hebrew term (kikkar) RKK, which means a disc or cycle. A whole circle of pagans worshipped the Sun as Baal or Lord, which is why pagans worshipped on Sun-day, the first day of the week, much as those who identify as Christians do now without realising they are pagan.

Circe and Her Swine - Briton Rivière (1840-1920)

Chapter 11: Mystery Babylonian Symbols - Extras

Mystery Babylonian Symbols - Extras

1. Pontifex Maximus

"The Bridge-Builder" is the official papal title of Pontifex Maximus, which is displayed on the floor of St. Peter's Basilica at the Vatican. Babylon is where this title first appeared. The religious ceremonies and traditions of Babylon were appropriated by Medo-Persia after they conquered it. Pontifex Maximus was the name given to their religious system by some of the Babylonian priests at Pergamum. After being passed down to pagan Roman emperors, the title, all of its accoutrements, and powers were finally seized by the Bishop of Rome. Additionally, take note of the winged lion, which is the biblical emblem for Babylon; the fleur-de-lis, which symbolises the union of male and female; the split tail, which symbolises the fish god Dagon; and the triple crown, which is connected to the Babylonian system.

2. All Seeing-Eye

'Eye and triangle' is the gold pectoral crucifix worn by John XXIII. Ancient Egypt is where the all-seeing-eye and even the concept of the trinity appeared.

3. Serpents and Occult Symbolism in Religion

Adam and Eve - Biblical Serpent

Lilith (with Satan the serpent), painting by John Collier (1892)

Bourdon, Sébastien - Moses and the Brazen Serpent (Julius Schnorr von Carolsfeld 1851-60)

Baphomet - Serpent Crosier

Serpent Crosier Christianity

Greek Orthodox Monastery in Mount Athos, Greece

All-seeing eye of Horus, in a Catholic church. Coming out of the Sun.

Mormon - 5 Pointed Pentagrams

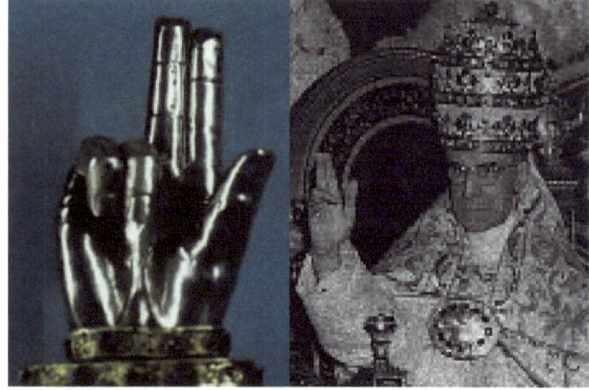

On thousands of statues and paintings all over the Vatican and in countless cathedrals and Roman Catholic churches worldwide, Satanic hand gestures from pagan Rome can be seen.

4. Babylonian Symbolism - Catholic Church

Symbol of Babylonian Sun-god Shamash

Ishtar Symbol (Venus)

Decorative Wheel Found On The Altar of a Roman Catholic Church

5. The Obelisk - The Vatican

A smaller four-pointed Sun wheel, which is the same sign as the altar stone of the temple of Baal in Hatzor, is located in the middle of the enormous eight-point Sun wheel encircling the obelisk in this old photograph of the centre of St. Peter's Square.

Pagan Sun worship is symbolised by the Egyptian obelisk in the middle of St. Peter's Square, the symbol of Baal inside the symbol of Ishtar. The obelisk is also identified as Osiris's phallus, which is his reproductive organ.

6. Babylonian Symbolism

The cross has pagan origins and is not a Christian symbol. Look at the cross on this Babylonian deities chest. The cross worn by Ashur-Nasir-Pal II, King of Assyria, is identical to the Maltese cross, which represents the Knights Templar.

Take note of King Ashur-Nasir-Pal II lower hand on the stele above. The sunburst symbol is worn on the wrist. Below, Pope John XXIII's glove bears the pagan sunburst.

7. Vatican Gold Coin and Ciborium

Vatican gold coin worth 100 Lire. Take note of the symbol of Baal, which is located in Hazor, behind the head of the Christ-figure.

Two ciborium specimens, where the Eucharistic wafer hosts of the Catholic Mass are kept, are seen on the left. The ancient symbols of Shamash and Baal, the four-pointed cross inside a circle, are used in the one on the left, while the Cross Pattée is used as the handle on top of the other.

8. Statue of St. Peter

The Sun wheel over his head, do you notice? Some people believe that this monument is originally a pagan statue of Jupiter that was taken from the Pantheon, a pagan temple in Rome, and relocated to St. Peter's; it was given the new name Peter. Numerous pilgrims have kissed the outstretched right foot in remembrance, till it has almost worn away. The sign of Baal/Shamash is also used in the pattern on the wall behind the statue

9. Fish Hat

The fish-headed mitre originated with 'Dagon' worshippers about 300 A.D. His symbol was a fish-mouth cap with a long piece of fabric that hung over the wearer's back and was painted or embroidered to resemble a fish's body. They initially even preserved the small dots on either side of the "fish head," which stood in for the eyes of the fish. You may believe that the mitre world's fishiness has been suppressed throughout time. Nevertheless, the fish head metaphor is still clearly visible in these Roman Catholic pictures.

Pope Paul VI - wearing the Judaic "Kohen Breastplate,"

10. Birds Of The Same Feathers

1) Ankh Nes Meryre and Son Pepi. 2) Cyprus. 3) Madonna Guanyin, Goddess of Mercy 4) Matrika from Tanesara of India 5) Yasoda and Krishna. 6) Mother and Son 2000-1850 B.C. 7) Mexico, Jalisco 200 B.C.- 500 A.D. 8) Maya. 9) Mexico, Colima 200 B.C.- 500A.D. 10) Mykene, Greece 11) Sun Goddess, Arinna. 12) Virgin Mary

11. Evolution of Sun Worship

From the top left: The Sun-god Apollo; the pagan Sun-god Shamash; Mithra, the Sol Invictus; From bottom left: The golden child in the Vatican palace; the Sun image in Baldacchino; and the pagan symbol in the Papal Palace Hall.

The fish god Dagon, the ancient fertility goddess Astarte, the ancient Egyptian mitre, the stone relief on an Assyrian temple laver at the Pergamon Museum in Berlin, and the bishop's mitre are seen from top left.

12. Pagan Cone to Papal Cone

The Mexican god holds the pine cone and the fur tree, symbols of rebirth and the Sun; Hindu god holds cone; the pine cone staff, symbol of Osiris; Assyrian winged god with pine cone; Bacchus, Roman-Greek god of drunkenness and revelry, with pine cone staff; Papal cone; The largest pine cone in the world, in the Court of the Pine Cone, at the Vatican, Rome.

13. The Tiara

Babylonian god wearing the triple crown; Assyrian winged-bull cherubim; Krishna with tiara.; Pope wears a tiara.

14. Avian Procession

In the past, Horus' messengers would be carried. As you can see on the right, they had fans that were fashioned to resemble eyes out of peacock feathers, which is hay that resembles a news station logo. This eye is Horus/Osiris's all-seeing eye. The Papacy follows the same tradition to the left.

15. From Serpent Gods to Vatican Serpents

The snake gods of Egypt, Rome, the Mayans, the Bishop's serpent crosier, and the new St. Mary's Cathedral in San Francisco, California, all have serpent door handles. On a big papal crest is a dragon.

16. The Halo

17. Symbol of Power

The crooks of Athena, the Egyptian divine-king, Osiris, a Catholic bishop, and a Catholic serpent-crook are all held in place.

18. Divide and Conquer

19. Grand Lodge of Freemasonry - Israel

The three major monotheistic religions' symbols—the Islamic Crescent, the Jewish Star of David, and the Christian Cross—are entwined inside the square and compasses of the Grand Lodge's official seal. This logo incorporates the cult of the Sun, Moon, and Saturn. I can assure you that both the elites and the founding fathers of Freemasonry are well aware of it.

20. Teotihuacan & Vatican Comparison

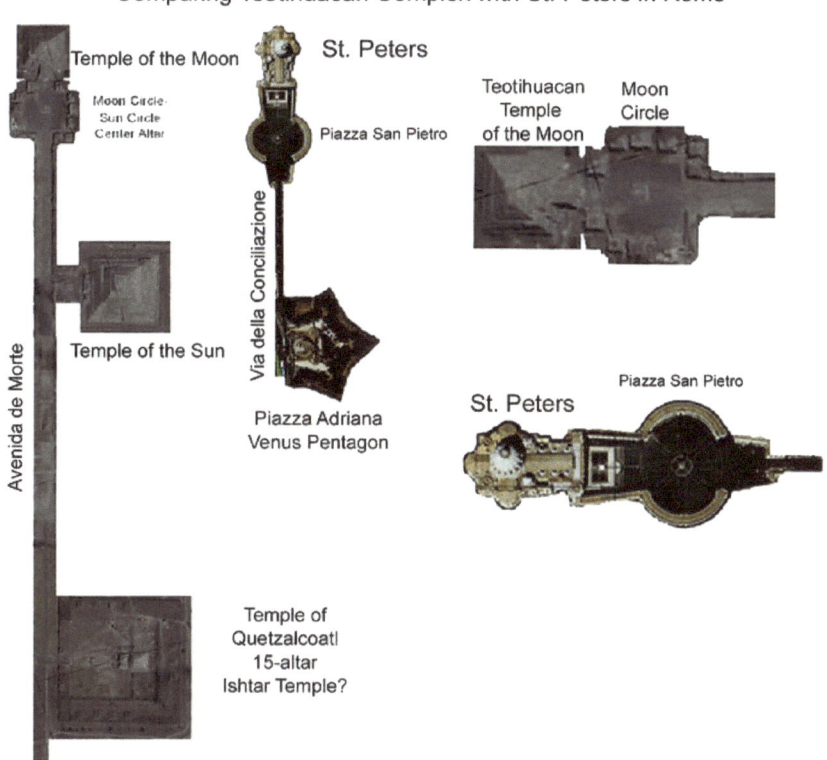

Closing

The content of this work aimed to provide readers another perspective on the origins of our major religious ideas. I am aware that there have been a lot of questions concerning the origins of these stories. The ability to distinguish between what's right and wrong, or discernment, is what matters. After reading this, I encourage readers to explore our distant religions on their own and see what they can find. We have been compelled to accept myths as facts for thousands of years, and people have painted a certain image of God. Numerous religions assert that their god is the one, all-powerful reality of all that exists. But it is only our flesh and egos that separate us from one another. Each of us is a unique drop in the vast ocean of consciousness. Energy is consciousness, and the body is dead as soon as consciousness is dead. Although infinite consciousness might be referred to as God, this is not the God that exists in our religions. God or Infinite Consciousness is a neutral energy that underpins all things, both visible and invisible.

We all perceive our Creation as Man, and we are all facets or expressions of the Infinite Consciousness. With our thoughts, we, as embodiments of the Infinite Consciousness that we are, construct the physical reality. Thus, we are Consciousness or God, and everything is it. As soon as we are separated, we start to distance ourselves from one another, play opposing positions and harbour animosity towards one another. And this is the reality that the ruling elites imposed on humanity after realising that they could maintain our division by introducing a hidden deity that held their purported one and only truth.

God or the infinite awareness on this planet is neutral, and the truth is objective. It does not support any one race or set of believers, nor does it take sides. Despite the claims made by many of these religious cults, there is no such thing as superior human beings or God's chosen people. Those who attain spirituality through love, peace, and positivity are accompanied by God, which stays still in the divine presence. The universe has already given us the solutions and the road map for navigating the Earth and bringing people together. Our current system hasn't worked for decades; on the contrary, it's time to reconsider and piece things together. If we all stop participating and giving these elitists power and control, their game is over. However, it is fear and false hope that are preventing the majority from implementing change and taking action.

References

- Philip Gardiner, "Gateways To The Otherworld"

- Origin of Language and Myths: Volume 1, Margan Peter Kavanagh

- The Christian Examiner, Fames Miller, Volumes 61-62

- A New System Or an Analysis of Ancient Mythology: Jacob Bryant Astrology Revelation 2

- A Descriptive Catalogue of a General Collection......., Volume 1, By Rudolf Erich Raspe, James Tassie, Pg. 217

- The New Strong's Exhaustive Concordance of the Bible - James Strong

- Historic Magazine and Notes and Queries, Volume 23, (1905), Pg. 130

- The Pentateuch and Book of Joshua Critically Examined: Bishop John William Colenso

- Tony Bushby: The Bible Fraud

- A Dissertation On The Ruins Or Revolutions Of Empires: R. J. Rowe, (1832), Pg. 220

- Isaiah 14:12 & "Kokab" http://biblehub.com/hebrew/3556.him

- The International Standard Bible Encyclopedia, Vol. 2: James Orr, pg. 800

- The Theosophical Glossary, Helena Petrovna Blavatsky, (1892), pg. 192

- Leisure Readings, edited by Richard Anthony Proctor, pg. 249

- Pamphlets, Religious: Miscellaneous, Volume 14, pg. 51

- Britannia Antiquissima; Or, A Key to the Philology of History (Sacred and Profane), Vol. I: John Jones Thomas, pg. 143

- Ancient Faiths Embodied in Ancient Names: Or, An Attempt to Trace ..., Volume 1, Thomas Inman, Pg. 173

- The Christian mythology unveiled, Logan Mitchell, Pg. 144

- Testimony of the Ages: Herbert William Morris, Enoch Fitch Burr, (1883), Pg. 953

- Historic Magazine and Notes and Queries:, Volume 12, (1894), Pg. 330-331

- The Comet, Volumes 1-2, Pg. 186* 330**

- The Œdipus Judaicus, sir William Drummond, Pg. 255

- Historic Magazine and Notes and Queries:, Volume 13, (1894), Pg. 216

- The Theosophical Glossary, Helena Petrovna Blavatsky, (1892), Pg. 374

- The Evolution of Man: His Religious Systems and Social Customs, William Wright Hardwicke, Pg. 81–82

- The Unitarian Review, Volume 35, (1891), Pg. 285-286

- Transactions of the Society of Biblical Archæology, Volumes 6-7,

- Society of Biblical Archæology (1878), Pg. 586

- From Chrishna to Christ, Raymond W. Bernard, Pg. 29

- Knowledge...: A Monthly Record of Science, Volume 27, Pg. xv

- Symbols, Sex, and the Stars, Ernest Busenbark, (1997), Pg. 149-150

- Dissertation on The ruins, or revolutions of empires: R. J. Rowe, (1832), Pg. 220-221

- Anacalypsis an Attempt to Draw Aside the Veil of the Saitic Isis ..., Volume 2, Godfrey Higgins, Pg. 112

- The Great Dionysiak Myth, Volume 1, Robert Brown, Pg. 59

- Book III Learning the Qabalah of the Et Custosi Tutelae, Freedman & Cabalis, Pg. 355

- The Herald of Progress, Pg. 210

- The Horned Altar: Rediscovering & Rekindling Canaanite Magic, Tess Dawson, Pg. 98

- The Alphabet: An Account of the Origin and Development of Letters, Volume 2, Isaac Taylor, Pg. 87

- "The Gods of the great ages" http:--the-red-thread.net-Gods-of-the-Ages.html

- "Bible Dates" http: www.usbible.com-Astrology-bible_dates.htm

- The Greek Rabalah: Alphabetical Mysticism and Numerology in the Ancient World: Kieren Barry, Pg.83

- The Mithraic Origin and meanings of the Rotas-Sator Square by Moeller, Walter O

- The Celtic Druids: Godfrey Higgins, Pg. 127

- Bible Myths and Their Parallels in Other Religions: Thomas William Dane, Pg, 349

Secondary Sources

- "Archaeological Photo Gallery of the Arabian Moon-God." Bible.ca, 2025, www.bible.ca/islam/islam-photos-Moon-worship-archealolgy.htm. Accessed 3 Feb. 2025.

- "Rome's Islam." Ssremnant.org, 2025, ssremnant.org/romeislam.html. Accessed 3 Feb. 2025.

- "ALLAH, the Moon God." Mikeblume.com, 2025, mikeblume.com/Moongod.htm. Accessed 3 Feb. 2025.

- "ᛟUN of ᛟATURN." YouTube, Accessed 3 Feb. 2025.

- Eoht.info, 2025, www.eoht.info/page/Abraham. Accessed 3 Feb. 2025.

- Thegreaterawakening.org, 2025, www.thegreaterawakening.org/church. Accessed 3 Feb. 2025.

- "Religious Luciferian Symbols." Whale.to, 2025, www.whale.to/c/churches_ill.html. Accessed 3 Feb. 2025.

- "Paganism – the WATCHMAN'S CRY." THE WATCHMAN'S CRY, 2020, freespirit16.wordpress.com/category/roman-catholicism/paganism/. Accessed 3 Feb. 2025.